THE

3-MINUTE

recharge

DEVOTIONAL

FOR WOMEN

365 Bible Readings to

Rejuvenate Your Spirit

THE

3-MINUTE
recharge
DEVOTIONAL
FOR WOMEN

365 Bible Readings to

Rejuvenate Your Spirit

BARBOUR
PUBLISHING

Published by Barbour Publishing, Inc., 1810 Barbour Drive, Uhrichsville, Ohio 44683, www.barbourbooks.com

Our mission is to inspire the world with the life-changing message of the Bible.

Member of the
Evangelical Christian
Publishers Association

Printed in China.

The LORD. . .
lets me rest in green meadows;
he leads me beside peaceful streams.
He renews my strength.
He guides me along right paths,
bringing honor to his name.

PSALM 23:1-3 NLT

Introduction

In just 3 minutes you can recharge your spirit!

These devotions were written especially for those moments when you need a little reminder that your heavenly Father offers You encouragement and inspiration—today and every day. Just 3 short minutes will help to refresh and renew your spirit as He does a new work in you.

Minute 1: Read the day's Bible verse and reflect on its meaning.

Minute 2: Read the devotional and think about its application to your life.

Minute 3: Pray.

Although these devotions aren't meant as a tool for deep Bible study, they can be a touch point to keep you rooted in and focused on God, who listens to your every prayer. May each moment you spend with this book be a blessing!

"Happy Eternally After"

Thine eyes did see my substance, yet being unperfect; and in thy book all my members were written, which in continuance were fashioned, when as yet there was none of them.

PSALM 139:16 KJV

The story of your life is written one day at a time. Every choice you make influences the chapters yet to come. But one thing is certain—the ending. Your future was written the moment you chose to follow God. That means the end of your story here on earth is actually a brand-new beginning. It's a story with endless chapters, a "happy eternally after" where tears are history and true love never fails.

I trust You as I journey on this earth, Lord. I don't know all the future holds, but I do know that You hold my future. I trust Your unfailing love for me!

The Trees That Catch the Storm

Brothers and sisters, I could not address you as people who live by the Spirit but as people who are still worldly—mere infants in Christ. I gave you milk, not solid food, for you were not yet ready for it. Indeed, you are still not ready.

1 Corinthians 3:1–2 NIV

Think of the healthiest trees in the forest. . .they stretch toward the sun and spread their branches wide. But when the storms of life blow, those towering oaks often catch the brunt of the wind. The last thing the enemy wants is for you to grow in Christ. So, expect storms; be watchful and ready. But remember that we can stand strong like the oak. We can know peace in the midst of the gale. Christ is the strength in our branches and the light that gives us life!

Jesus, help me to grow strong in the rich, nourishing soil of Your love and grace. Make me an oak for Your cause. Amen.

Near at Hand

Quiet down before GOD, be prayerful before him.
PSALM 37:7 MSG

It's not easy to be quiet. Our world is loud, and the noise seeps into our hearts and minds. We feel restless and jumpy, on edge. God seems far away. But God is always near at hand, no matter how we feel. When we quiet our hearts, we will find Him there, patiently waiting, ready to show us His grace.

Lord, when my heart is restless and jumpy, remind me that You are near, waiting to comfort me with Your love. Quiet me with Your nearness. Show me Your grace. Amen.

Simply Love

But I am giving you a new command.
You must love each other, just as I have loved you.
JOHN 13:34 CEV

Christ doesn't ask us to point out others' faults. He doesn't require that we be the morality squad, focusing on all that is sinful in the world around us. Instead, He wants us to simply love, just as He loves us. When we do, the world will see God's grace shining in our lives.

Jesus, there is such simplicity in merely loving others with Your love. Help me to follow this new command and let the world see Your grace shining in my life. Amen.

Even More!

*Now unto him that is able to do exceeding
abundantly above all that we ask or think,
according to the power that worketh in us.*

EPHESIANS 3:20 KJV

"Above all that we ask or think" is just that. Imagine every good thing that God has promised in His Word—or things you've only dreamed about. Think of wonderful things that exceed the limits of human comprehension or description, then imagine that God is able and *willing* to do even more!

The last part of this verse indicates that the Holy Spirit works within the Christian's life to accomplish the seemingly impossible. Our highest aspirations are within God's power—but like Paul, we must pray. When we do, God does far more for us than we could ever guess.

Oh Lord, You accomplish things I perceive
as impossible. You know my hopes and
dreams, and I believe that You are able to
exceed my greatest expectations. Amen.

Thanksgiving Sacrifices

*You called out to GOD in your desperate condition;
he got you out in the nick of time. He spoke the word
that healed you, that pulled you back from the brink
of death. So thank GOD for his marvelous love, for his
miracle mercy to the children he loves; offer thanksgiving
sacrifices, tell the world what he's done—sing it out!*

PSALM 107:18–22 MSG

We think of sacrifice as "giving up something." Originally, *sacrifice* meant "to offer something to God." The sacrifice God wants most from us is that of thanksgiving, because by offering our gratitude to God, we enrich our lives. We see God's mercy at work in our world. We expand our sense of joy. We realize the reality of His marvelous love. So sing it out! Don't keep it to yourself. Tell the world all the amazing things God has done.

God, I want to offer You a sacrifice of thanksgiving.
May I not save this sacrifice for special occasions,
but instead may it be my daily practice.

Honorable

[God] loves it when business is aboveboard.
PROVERBS 11:1 MSG

Whether you're a stay-at-home mother, empty-nester, CEO, student, teacher, or attorney, God expects you to be honest in all your transactions—at the grocery store, the local bank, with your children and husband, in the boardroom, in court, on your tax forms, and when interacting with your repairman. Maybe you had trustworthy role models when you were growing up; perhaps you didn't. But as an aspiring wise woman, you can keep your everyday business dealings honorable. God will help.

Lord, please cultivate my heart to become
a woman of integrity. Teach me to see that
all my actions and transactions can be good,
honest work—work that honors You.

Trusting

A prudent person foresees danger and takes precautions.
PROVERBS 22:3 NLT

Wisdom means planning for the worst, anticipating the best, and trusting God with every outcome. Whether you're researching colleges to attend, purchasing a home, getting married, starting a new company, taking care of your aging parents, or have just learned you're pregnant, you'll want to ask intelligent questions and plan for your next steps. God encourages you to think ahead. Seek the advice of trusted friends and associates, take necessary precautions, and then turn the results over to Him.

Heavenly Father, I need Your wisdom as I plan
for the future. Help me to see my life as Yours.
I trust You to help me make the next wise choice.

God Is at Work

The lines are fallen unto me in pleasant
places; yea, I have a goodly heritage.
PSALM 16:6 KJV

It's been said that we don't know what the future holds, but we know who holds the future. Tomorrow is not a potluck of chance possibilities. The Bible tells us that God is at work, bringing something good out of every situation His children face. Knowing a God who deeply loves us and is in control, no matter what comes our way, allows us to hold our heads high and walk toward the future with confident expectation.

My only hope is in You, Lord. My confidence is in You. My faith is in You. I am so thankful that I can trust You with my life.

The Abundant Life

Thou hast put gladness in my heart, more than in the time that their corn and their wine increased.
PSALM 4:7 KJV

An "abundant life" is not something we can pick up at the mall or purchase online. It comes from recognizing how much we receive from God each and every day. While some of our abundance may come in the form of possessions, the overflow of an abundant life ultimately comes from what fills our hearts, not our closets. Resting in God's "more-than-enough" can transform a desire to acquire into a prayer of thanksgiving for what we've already been given.

Your Word tells me that You fill me with joy in Your presence. Continue to put gladness in my heart, Lord. Show me how to be content with what You've given me.

What to Do with Free Will

> *"If you do what is right, will you not be accepted?*
> *But if you do not do what is right, sin is crouching at your*
> *door; it desires to have you, but you must rule over it."*
> GENESIS 4:7 NIV

Every single thing we do every minute of the day involves a choice, and everything has a ripple effect. Everything has consequences. What we eat for breakfast. What books we read, what programs we watch on television Where we go, what we spend our time and money on. Sin is always crouching at our door, but with the help of the Holy Spirit, we can ask it to leave. What will your choices be today?

Holy Spirit, guide me in my decisions.
Help me to be wise, clearheaded, and motivated
by a selfless love for You and others. Amen.

The Right People

The Lord God said, "It isn't good for the man to live alone. I will make a suitable partner for him."
GENESIS 2:18 CEV

God understands that human beings need each other. His love comes to us through others. That is the way He designed us, and we can trust His grace to bring the right people along when we need them, the people who will banish our loneliness and share our lives.

———————

God, thank You for creating me to live in harmony with other people. Thank You for showing me Your love through others. Help me to love them well. Amen.

Rejoice!

Rejoice in the Lord always. I will say it again: Rejoice!
PHILIPPIANS 4:4 NIV

When God is the source of our joy, we will never lose that joy. Circumstances may frustrate us and break our hearts, but God is able to supply all our needs. He is able to restore broken relationships. He can give us a new job or help us to succeed at our current job. Through it all, despite it all, we can rejoice in knowing that we are God's and He loves us.

———————————

Dear Father, thank You for loving me.
Help me to make You the source of my joy. Amen.

All the Lonely People

Be devoted to one another in love.
Honor one another above yourselves.
ROMANS 12:10 NIV

As Christians, let's keep an eye out for those lonely souls, the people who need a smile and a helping hand. Those who need a cup of cool water and a listening ear—who need a friend. Let us open our hearts and homes to them. As the book of Romans reminds us, "Be devoted to one another in love. Honor one another above yourselves." This is God's cure for all the lonely people. Amazingly enough, when we reach out to lessen someone else's lonesomeness, perhaps we will ease our own.

Father, give me the desire to live my life for You
and for everyone around me. Deepen and enrich
my relationships with family and friends. Amen.

Be Encouraged

The diligent find freedom in their work.
PROVERBS 12:24 MSG

It's fun watching a juggler. He tosses and balances balls, knives, hats, and sometimes flaming torches. It appears easy. Yet if you asked, you'd probably discover how many focused and diligent hours he practices. Learning to work without the constant buzz of busyness is like learning a juggling act. Although you want to stop rushing, it feels so impossible that you're tempted to cease trying. But be encouraged. You'll find success if you stay committed to practicing a balanced schedule.

Father, teach me to be diligent as I seek Your
will for my life. Show me what's important
and where I need to persevere. Help me find
balance as I live out Your purposes.

Praying in Expectation

The eyes of all wait upon thee; and thou
givest them their meat in due season.
PSALM 145:15 KJV

Praying without expecting God to answer is kind of like wishing on a star. You don't believe it's going to make any difference, but you do it anyway—just in case there really is something behind all those fairy tales. When you pray, do so with great expectations. God is at work on behalf of a child He dearly loves—you. Just remember, God's answers may arrive in ways and at a time that you least expect.

Your Word tells me that prayer is powerful and effective. I trust in You, Lord. I trust that You have my best interests at heart as You answer my prayers.

Grateful Generosity

A good man sheweth favour, and lendeth:
he will guide his affairs with discretion.
PSALM 112:5 KJV

A funny thing happens when you get in the habit of sharing what God has given you. The more you give, the more you realize how blessed you are and the more grateful you become—which inspires you to share even more of what you have with others. It's a wonderful cycle that loosens your grip on material things so both your hands and your heart can more freely reach out to those around you.

———————

I offer up everything I have to You, Lord. It all belongs to You anyway. Lead me to bless others with what You have given me. Help me to show love in tangible ways.

The Better You Know God

The Lord preserveth the simple:
I was brought low, and he helped me.
PSALM 116:6 KJV

Feel like you need more faith? Sometimes what we really need is the courage to act on what we already believe. A skydiver may have faith her parachute is packed correctly, but that doesn't stop her stomach from doing its own loop-de-loop as she jumps out of the plane. However, the more she dives, the less nervous she feels. The better you know God, the more a leap of faith feels like a hop into your loving Father's waiting arms.

———————————

Just as the man talking to Jesus said, "Lord,
I believe. Help my unbelief," I want to believe more
too, Lord. Fill me with a desire to know You more.

Gift of Faith

*Lead me in thy truth, and teach me: for thou art the
God of my salvation; on thee do I wait all the day.*
PSALM 25:5 KJV

Faith is both a gift we receive and an action we take. God's Spirit
gives us enough faith to reach out to a Father we cannot see. But
as we continue reaching—continue putting our trust in God as
we go through life—that little gift of faith grows stronger, like
a muscle consistently put to work at the gym. Give your faith a
workout today by doing what you believe God wants you to do.

Help me live by faith and not by sight, Lord.
You've already provided all the evidence
I need. I look at the world and people
around me, and I see Your handiwork.

The Time Is Now

But God demonstrates his own love for us in this:
While we were still sinners, Christ died for us.
ROMANS 5:8 NIV

In the book of Mark, Jesus said, "The time has come. . . . The kingdom of God has come near. Repent and believe the good news!" (Mark 1:15). Have you embraced this good news? The kingdom of God has come near to you. Why are you waiting? The time is now. Ask the Lord for forgiveness and be free. Believe in Him as Lord and be made right with God. Accept His grace and live with the Lord for all time. Oh, yes, what a joy—to know love the way it was meant to be!

Thank You, Lord Jesus, that even while I was deep in my sin, You gave up your life so that I might truly live. What a sacrifice. What a Savior! Thank You for Your unfathomable mercy, Your immeasurable love. Amen.

Turning Bondage into Balance

*It is for freedom that Christ has set us free.
Stand firm, then, and do not let yourselves
be burdened again by a yoke of slavery.*
GALATIANS 5:1 NIV

The Lord wants us to have a sound mind, which means finding balance in life. How can we be warm, giving, creative, fun, and a light to the world if we are frozen solid in an unmovable block of perfectionism? Let Jesus melt the block of bondage that says, "Never good enough," and let us be able to shout the words, "It is good, and it is finished. Praise God!"

Lord, help me not to be a slave to perfectionism, but in all things, let me find balance and joy. Amen.

He Won't Let You Down

I tell you that Christ has become a servant of the Jews on behalf of God's truth, so that the promises made to the patriarchs might be confirmed.
ROMANS 15:8 NIV

Everyone has been hurt at one time or another by a broken promise. When that happens, it is best to forgive and go on. People are just people. They mess up. But there is one who will never break His promises to us—our heavenly Father. We can safely place our hope in Him. Choose to place your hope in God's promises. You won't be discouraged by time—God's timing is always perfect. You won't be discouraged by circumstances—God can change everything in a heartbeat. He is faithful.

Lord, I choose this day to place my trust in You for I know You're the one, true constant. Amen.

Unshakable

*For the LORD is good; his mercy is everlasting;
and his truth endureth to all generations.*
PSALM 100:5 KJV

With time, we come to believe certain things are unshakable. The sun rises and sets. The tides ebb and flow. Seasons revolve year after year. Babies are born, people die, and the world goes on pretty much as it has for centuries: faithful to a predictable pattern. But there will come a time when the world as we know it will end. Only God is totally unshakable and unchanging. His love and goodness to us will remain forever faithful.

Lord, You are good to me, and I trust Your promises. I give You any doubts and fears about my future, and I trust Your heart for Your people.

Faithful Love

*Hallelujah! Give thanks to the Lord,
for He is good; His faithful love endures forever.*
PSALM 106:1 HCSB

Even the most devoted spouse or oldest friend can let us down.
They may not mean to or want to, but humans make mistakes;
they're not perfect, and it would be unrealistic to expect them to
be. That doesn't keep our feelings from being hurt, though! And
it hurts even worse when people we love intentionally turn their
backs on us. But God will never do that. Unlike human beings,
He has no limits to His love. His faithfulness endures forever.
And that's good reason to thank Him!

Thank You, dearest Lord, for Your love
that never fails. Thank You that no matter
what happens, I can rely on You.

Equipped to Do God's Will

May the God of peace, who through the blood of the eternal covenant brought back from the dead our Lord Jesus, that great Shepherd of the sheep, equip you with everything good for doing his will, and may he work in us what is pleasing to him, through Jesus Christ, to whom be glory for ever and ever. Amen.
HEBREWS 13:20–21 NIV

Hebrews says God will work in us what is pleasing to Him. When He is at work in you, you may be stretched mentally, emotionally, physically, and spiritually to new places. The good news is that He provides you with everything you need. Like a good football coach wants his team to succeed, God wants His children to receive the blessing of living in His perfect will. You are equipped for the ride!

Father, I ask that You equip me
to do Your will in my life.

Get Real

*The Lord says: "These people come near to me with
their mouth and honor me with their lips, but their
hearts are far from me. Their worship of me is based
on merely human rules they have been taught."*

ISAIAH 29:13 NIV

The world is full of hypocrites and sometimes the church is
too. They profess to know and honor God, but they are only
going through the motions of religion. Their hearts are far
from Him. Take the time to find out who God is, what He
has done for you, and why He is worthy of your devotion.
Following God is not about a bunch of man-made rules. He
loves you; He sent His Son to die for you; and He longs to have
a deep, personal relationship with you. Get real with God and
with yourself!

Dear God, reveal Yourself to me. Show me who You
are, and show me how to live so that I honor You not
only with my lips but with my heart as well. Amen.

Loving Generosity

The wicked borroweth, and payeth not again:
but the righteous sheweth mercy, and giveth.
PSALM 37:21 KJV

Love and generosity are two sides of the same coin. Both put the needs of others before their own. Both give without expecting anything in return. Both make our invisible God more visible to a world in need. As our love for those around us grows, generosity can't help but follow suit. Today, become more aware of the needs of those around you. Then ask God to help you act on what you see with loving generosity.

Lord, every time I have given unselfishly, You pour more blessings back into my life. The greatest blessing of all is Your presence in my life.

Keeping Our Promises

What shall I return to the LORD for all his goodness to me? I will lift up the cup of salvation and call on the name of the LORD. I will fulfill my vows to the LORD in the presence of all his people. . . . I will sacrifice a thank offering to you and call on the name of the LORD. I will fulfill my vows to the LORD in the presence of all his people.
PSALM 116:12–14, 17–18 NIV

One way we can express our gratitude to God is by keeping our promises to Him. But God doesn't expect us to do this alone. We have the support of God's people and His Spirit within us, setting us free for God's service. With that help, we can keep our promises to God, offering Him a sacrifice of thanksgiving and love.

Set me free, Lord, so I can serve You.
I am so grateful for all You have done for me.

Nature

Sing to GOD a thanksgiving hymn, play music on your instruments to God, who fills the sky with clouds, preparing rain for the earth, then turning the mountains green with grass, feeding both cattle and crows.

PSALM 147:7–9 MSG

Sometimes we take the world of nature for granted. As the seasons cycle, it's all just the background for our busy lives. But the Bible reminds us to pause and truly *see* God's hand at work in nature. From the rain that turns the earth green, to the majestic mountains, to the earth's beasts, to the ever-changing beauty of the clouds in the sky, our world is filled with loveliness. God has created a world of vast beauty. When we remember to look around us and truly appreciate the world of nature, our hearts will spill over with gratitude to the one who created it all.

Thank You, Creator God, for the beautiful world You have given us. Help us to care for it responsibly.

I Think I Can

"Do not be afraid; only believe."
MARK 5:36 NKJV

Take a trip through the Bible and you'll see that those God asked to do the impossible were ordinary people of their day, yet they demonstrated that they believed God saw something in them that they didn't see. He took ordinary men and women and used them to do extraordinary things. When you believe you can do something, your faith goes to work. You rise to the challenge, which enables you to go further than before, to do more than you thought possible. Consider trying something new—if you think you can, you can!

God, I want to have high expectations. I want to do more than most think I can do. Help me to reach higher and do more as You lead me. Amen.

Beside You—Always

*No need to panic over alarms or surprises, or predictions
that doomsday's just around the corner, because GOD will
be right there with you; he'll keep you safe and sound.*
PROVERBS 3:25–26 MSG

Everyone feels fearful at times. What if I lose my job? What if
the terrorists strike again? What if I get sick and can't take care
of my family? None of us want these things to happen. Yet when
we focus on the what-ifs, rationality and common sense often
go out the window. God, the wisdom giver, is also your protec-
tor. He is right beside you always. You can trust Him with this
moment—and with your future.

Forgive me for worrying about the future, Lord.
You tell me that it's senseless to do so and
rids my life of joy in the present moment.

What's in Your Heart?

Delight thyself also in the LORD:
and he shall give thee the desires of thine heart.
PSALM 37:4 KJV

Too many times we look at God's promises as some sort of magic formula. We fail to realize that His promises have more to do with our own relationship with Him. It begins with a heart's desire to live your life in a way that pleases God. Only then will fulfillment of His promises take place. The promise in Psalm 37:4 isn't intended for personal gain—it is meant to glorify God. God wants to give you the desires of your heart when they line up with His perfect plan. As you delight in Him, His desires will become your desires, and you will be greatly blessed.

Lord, I know You want to give me the desires of my heart. Help me live in a way that makes this possible.

Owning Your Faith

"But the Helper, the Holy Spirit, whom the Father will send in My name, He will teach you all things, and bring to your remembrance all things that I said to you."
JOHN 14:26 NKJV

Is your faith deeper and stronger than when you first accepted Jesus? While we are responsible for choosing to grow in faith, we can't do it on our own. Jesus promises that the Holy Spirit will teach and guide us if we allow Him to. He will help us remember the spiritual truths we've learned over the years. Fellowship with other Christians also helps us to mature as we share our passions and are encouraged. God wants you to own your faith. Make it real with words and actions.

Jesus, I want to know You intimately. Help me to mature in my walk with You daily. Guide my steps as I seek You through Your Word. Amen.

Wonderful!

Commit your actions to the LORD,
and your plans will succeed.
PROVERBS 16:3 NLT

Just because we want something to happen doesn't mean it will, no matter how hard we pray. We've all found that out (often to our sorrow!). But when we truly commit everything we do to God, praying only for His grace to be given free rein in our lives, then we will be surprised by what comes about. It may not be what we imagined—but it will be wonderful!

———————————

Father, Your Word tells me that Your ways are not my ways. I pray that I would graciously commit all my plans to You, armed with the promise that You will help them succeed. Amen.

Safe with Him

The name of the LORD is a strong fortress;
the godly run to him and are safe.
PROVERBS 18:10 NLT

Stop. Pause. Breathe. Take a moment to contemplate how big God is. How He orchestrates nature by His power. That right now He is with you and with your friend across the ocean. How He never sleeps yet doesn't tire. Think how much He loves you. How He sent Jesus to prove that love. Let your heart run to Him. Sense His strong arms holding you. Pray, telling Him what you're feeling at this moment. You're safe with Him.

Lord, You are my place of true safety. I run to You,
and I know You can handle everything I bring.
Thank You for Your great love and protection.

God's Gentleness

Teach me to do thy will; for thou art my God:
thy spirit is good; lead me into the land of uprightness.
PSALM 143:10 KJV

God doesn't drag His children through life by the wrist like a domineering parent with a self-centered agenda. God leads with love, gently and quietly. God's Spirit whispers, "Go this way," as a verse of scripture crosses your mind. He tenderly nudges your conscience toward making good choices and reaching out in love. He brings comfort in countless creative ways that those who don't recognize Him label as coincidence. God's gentleness reminds us that His power is always tempered by love.

Your Word tells us that we can hear and know
Your voice, Lord. Quiet my mind to hear Your
voice more clearly. I want to follow You.

God's Gates

Shout triumphantly to the LORD, all the earth.
Serve the LORD with gladness; come before Him
with joyful songs. Acknowledge that Yahweh is God.
He made us, and we are His—His people, the sheep of
His pasture. Enter His gates with thanksgiving and His
courts with praise. Give thanks to Him and praise His
name. For Yahweh is good, and His love is eternal;
His faithfulness endures through all generations.
PSALM 100:1–5 HCSB

This is "a psalm of thanksgiving." It outlines how we enter the gates leading into God's presence—through praise, service, song, gratitude. These are the entry points into the times and places where we feel His presence most deeply. He has given us so many reasons to feel thankful!

Dear Lord, help me to serve You with gladness;
teach me to sing Your name with songs of joy;
let me overflow with thanksgiving for all You have
done for me. Thank You that I am among the sheep
You care for. Thank You for Your faithfulness.

All You Need

"For your Maker is your husband—the LORD Almighty is his name—the Holy One of Israel is your Redeemer; he is called the God of all the earth."

ISAIAH 54:5 NIV

God is the great "I Am." He is all things that we need. He is our maker. He is our husband. He is the Lord Almighty, the Holy One, the Redeemer, the God of all the earth. . . . He is not a god made of stone or metal. He is not unreachable. He is present. He is near, as close as you will let Him be, and He will meet your needs as no earthly relationship can. Seek the fullness of God in your life. Call upon Him as your Prince of Peace and your King of Glory. He is all that you need—at all times—in all ways.

Oh Father, be close to me. Fill the empty
spots in my heart. Be my husband,
my redeemer, and my best friend. Amen.

Life and Nourishment

> "I, the LORD, am the one who answers your
> prayers and watches over you. I am like a green
> pine tree; your blessings come from me."
> HOSEA 14:8 NCV

Think of it: God is like a tree growing at the center of your life!
In the shade of this tree, you find shelter. This tree is evergreen,
with deep roots that draw up life and nourishment. Each one
of life's daily blessings is the fruit of this tree. It is the source of
all your life, all your joy, and all your being.

Lord, how can I thank You for answering my prayers
and watching over me? I am grateful for Your many
blessings and for You, the source of my being. Amen.

Every Step of the Way

Never stop praying.
1 Thessalonians 5:17 nlt

Several passages in the Bible tell us clearly that God listens to us when we pray. He hears every word and is compassionate. All we have to do is share our concerns with Him and wait faithfully for what He will provide.

God wants to be involved in our daily routines. He wants to hear from us and waits for us. God never promised an easy life to Christians. If we will allow Him, though, God will be there with us every step of the way. All we need to do is to come to Him in prayer. With these three simple words from 1 Thessalonians 5:17, our lives can be fulfilling as we live to communicate with our Lord.

Father, when I pray, remind me that prayer is not only about talking to You but also about listening to You. Open my heart to Your words. Amen.

Rebuilding

"I'll turn things around for Jacob. I'll compassionately
come in and rebuild homes. The town will be rebuilt on
its old foundations; the mansions will be splendid again.
Thanksgivings will pour out of the windows; laughter will
spill through the doors. Things will get better and better.
Depression days are over. They'll thrive, they'll flourish."
JEREMIAH 30:18–19 MSG

The Bible never promises that God's people will experience
unending success, wealth, and contentment. Instead, it makes
clear that all of us will have times when everything seems to be
falling apart. The "buildings" (whether they be actual homes or
relationships, family roles, or careers) that we constructed so
carefully and lovingly seem to fall down around us. But God
never leaves us in that state of ruin. The old foundations will
be used to build something new. We will laugh once again. We
will be thankful for all that God has done to rebuild our lives.

God of love, when everything seems to be falling
down, remind me that You always rebuild.

A Network of Love and Grace

For all things are for your sakes, so that grace,
having spread to more and more people, will cause
thanksgiving to overflow to the glory of God.
2 CORINTHIANS 4:15 NASB

All things are for our sake? Seems like an exaggeration, doesn't it? How can everything that happens be for us? But Paul, the author of the letter to the Corinthians, is saying that here. Elsewhere, he wrote that all things work together for good (Romans 8:28), and perhaps this is what he means here as well. What's good for me will also be good for you, and what's good for you isn't going to be bad for someone else. Somehow God knits everything together—even the difficult things, even the terrible things—into a network of love and grace that grows and spreads until more people are caught up into it.

Lord, make me an active participant in Your network of love—and I will spread thanksgiving to everyone I meet.

My Life

*I long for your salvation, Lord, and your law
gives me delight. Let me live that I may praise
you, and may your laws sustain me.*
Psalm 119:174–175 niv

Can you really do laundry to please God? Can you really go
to work to please God? Can you really pay the bills and make
dinner to please God? The answer is a resounding *yes!* Doing
all the mundane tasks of everyday life with gratitude and praise
in your heart for all that He has done for you is living a life of
praise. As you worship God through your day-to-day life, He
makes clear His plans, goals, and dreams for you.

Dear Father, let me live my life to praise You.
Let that be my desire each day. Amen.

By His Grace

A person is made right with God through
faith, not through obeying the law.
ROMANS 3:28 NCV

Human laws can never make us into the people we are meant to be. No matter how scrupulous we try to be, we will always fall short. Our hands and hearts will come up empty. But as we fix our eyes on God, committing our lives and ourselves to Him, we are made right. We are healed and made whole by His grace, exactly as God meant us to be.

———————

Father, rather than working to become righteous in Your sight, help me instead to focus on increasing my faith and trusting in Your grace. Amen.

God's Goodness

O fear the LORD, ye his saints:
for there is no want to them that fear him.
PSALM 34:9 KJV

In the Old Testament book of Exodus, we read about Moses, a man God referred to as "friend." When Moses asks to see God's glory, God shows Moses His goodness. Afterward, Moses' face literally glows. When we worship God, we glimpse His goodness. We focus on who He is, what He's done, and what He's promised is yet to come. Our faces may not glow like Moses', but glimpsing God's goodness is bound to bathe our hearts in joy.

Your Word tells me that those who look to You are radiant; their faces are never covered in shame. Thank You for filling me with Your Spirit, Lord God!

Giving Back

"Now therefore, our God, we thank You,
and praise Your glorious name."
1 CHRONICLES 29:13 NASB

The Hebrew word used for "thank" here in the original scripture is an interesting one. It came from a gesture that meant "to throw" or "to cast off." In other words, when we thank God for something, we don't hug it tight to our chest. In fact, we don't even claim it as our own. We give it back to the one who gave it to us. We don't insist on our right to control this gift, but instead we share it with God. Again and again in the Bible, praise and thanksgiving go hand in hand. We can't praise God without feeling gratitude for all He has done. And we can't do either without giving back to God all He has given to us.

———————————

Lord, You have given me so much.
Help me to give it all back to You.

The Whale's Belly

Jonah. . .prayed: "In trouble, deep trouble, I prayed
to God. He answered me. From the belly of the
grave I cried, 'Help!' You heard my cry. You threw
me into ocean's depths, into a watery grave. . . .
Yet you pulled me up from that grave alive, O God,
my God! . . . I'm worshiping you, God, calling out in
thanksgiving! And I'll do what I promised I'd do!"
JONAH 2:1–3, 6, 9 MSG

We all have times when we feel trapped somewhere small and
dark, deep in a sea of trouble, and we don't see a way out. Jonah
could have been angry with God, but his thoughts turned to
worship and thanksgiving. As always, thanksgiving was also an
act of surrender for Jonah. He would no longer rebel against
God's plan for his life but would go wherever God told him to go.

Lord, when I feel overwhelmed,
remind me to turn to You in thanksgiving,
with a new willingness to serve You.

No Matter What

Be thankful in all circumstances, for this is God's will for you who belong to Christ Jesus.
1 Thessalonians 5:18 nlt

Jesus enables us to be thankful, and Jesus is the cause of our thankfulness. *No matter what happens*, we know that Jesus has given up His life to save ours. He has sacrificed Himself on the cross so that we may live life to the fullest. And while "to the fullest" means that we will experience pain as well as joy, we must *always* be thankful—regardless of our circumstances—for the love that we experience in Christ Jesus.

Dear Lord, thank You for Your love. Please let me be thankful even in the midst of hardships. You have blessed me beyond measure. Amen.

Promises Kept

Thy kingdom is an everlasting kingdom, and thy dominion endureth throughout all generations.
PSALM 145:13 KJV

There's an old saying that warns, "Promises are made to be broken." With God, the opposite is true. The Bible is filled with promises God has made and kept. With a track record like that, it means you can trust God's Word and His love for you. He remains faithful even if your faithfulness to Him wavers from time to time. God and His promises have stood the test of time and will remain steadfast throughout eternity.

You are always faithful to me, Lord. You are the perfect parent, and Your love for me never wavers. I trust You with my life.

The Aroma of God

*Thanks be to God, who always leads us in triumph
in Christ, and through us reveals the fragrance
of the knowledge of Him in every place.*

2 CORINTHIANS 2:14 NASB

Some of us were brought up in churches where we were encouraged to "witness" to others about the salvation of Christ. Sometimes we got the idea that this witnessing had to be an unnatural sort of thing where we cornered poor hapless souls and hammered the way of salvation into their heads. In this verse, however, Paul is writing about a very different kind of witness. It's not something we do for God; it's something God just naturally does *through* us as we live in a relationship with Him. Everywhere we go, others will breathe the sweet scent of His presence—not because we're shoving it down their throats but because God is at work through us. Thanks be to God!

Dear Lord, draw me closer and closer to You
so that others will smell Your scent on me.

Helping Others

Carrying out this social relief work involves far more than helping meet the bare needs of poor Christians. It also produces abundant and bountiful thanksgivings to God. This relief offering is a prod to live at your very best, showing your gratitude to God by being openly obedient to the plain meaning of the Message of Christ. You show your gratitude through your generous offerings to your needy brothers and sisters, and really toward everyone.

2 Corinthians 9:12–13 msg

The Bible makes clear that we should be concerned with the souls of others and with their physical well-being. As we reach out in practical ways to those in need, whether emotionally or physically, we not only help them, we also express our gratitude to God for all He has done in our lives. We become part of an ever-growing network of love that spreads abundance and thanksgiving from our lives out into the world.

Lord, show me where and how I can
be of service to those in need.

Abide in the Vine

> *"I am the vine; you are the branches.*
> *If you remain in me and I in you, you will bear*
> *much fruit; apart from me you can do nothing."*
> JOHN 15:5 NIV

The fruit we bear is consistent with Christ's character. Just as apple trees bear apples, we bear spiritual fruit that reflects Him. Spiritual fruit consists of God's qualities: love, joy, peace, patience, kindness, goodness, faithfulness, gentleness, and self-control. The fruit of the spirit cannot be grown by our own efforts. We must remain in the vine. How do we abide in Him? We acknowledge that our spiritual sustenance comes from the Lord. We spend time with Him. We seek His will and wisdom. We are obedient and follow where He leads. Abide in the vine and be fruitful!

Dear Lord, help me abide in You so that I may produce fruit as a witness to Your life within me. Amen.

Safe

My life is in your hands. Save me from my
enemies and from those who are chasing me.
PSALM 31:15 NCV

Do you ever feel like trouble is chasing you? No matter how fast you run or how you try to hide, it comes relentlessly after you, dogging your footsteps, breathing its hot breath down your neck, robbing you of peace. What's even worse is that it waits for you down the road as well! Maybe you need to stop running and hiding and instead let yourself drop into God's hands, knowing He will hold your future safe.

Lord, when I am afraid, my instinct is to run.
Thank You for this reminder that my life is in Your
hands. Keep me safe. Help me to be still. Amen.

Something Good

O my soul, thou hast said unto the Lord,
Thou art my Lord: my goodness extendeth not to thee.
Psalm 16:2 kjv

What is good about your life? Consider how every good thing we receive can be tied back to God. Family. Friends. Talents. The ability to earn an income. It's easy to take the good things in our lives for granted, while readily putting the blame on God when we feel things go wrong. The next time you notice you're feeling happy about something good in your life, look for the part God played in sending it your way.

You are so good to me, Lord! You fill my life
with good things. I see Your hand in everything I
have. Thank You for the life You've given me.

Happiness Requirement

*I'm just as happy with little as with much,
with much as with little. . . . Whatever I have,
wherever I am, I can make it through anything
in the One who makes me who I am.*

PHILIPPIANS 4:12–13 MSG

When you were younger, what did you think you needed to be happy? Nice clothes? A boyfriend? A husband? A good job? At this point in your life, what is it you think your happiness requires? Day after day, God blesses us, but our happiness does not depend on those blessings. Our joy depends only on God. When we realize that, we no longer have to worry about losing or gaining life's blessings.

———

Jesus, giver of joy, help me to learn the secret of contentment. Help me to rest in the assurance that whatever life gives or takes away, I can always depend on You. Amen.

Spilling Over

*Our prayers for you are always spilling over
into thanksgivings. We can't quit thanking God
our Father and Jesus our Messiah for you!*
COLOSSIANS 1:3 MSG

The Bible tells us to pray for one another. As we lift each other's troubles and trials to God, we join God's work of love and empowerment. But we need not let our hearts be weighed down by others' pain and problems. Instead, our prayers can spill over into thanksgiving. We can be filled with expectation and hope, for although we don't know how God will answer our prayers, we do know that He *will*. God will do something amazing and marvelous in the lives of those we love—and gratitude affirms that reality.

———

Thank You, Lord, for all You are
doing in the lives of those I love.

United

I will give You thanks in the great congregation;
I will praise You among a mighty people
PSALM 35:18 NASB

Gratitude is a private, personal emotion. We experience it as individuals. But we can give expression to it in unity with others. Whether at church or in some other group that is doing God's work, when we lift our hearts and voices with others, we will find that we are strengthened and encouraged. Our own heart's thanksgiving expands and joins with others' praise. It's a little like singing: one voice alone is beautiful, but a chorus of many voices can make us feel as though we are experiencing a little bit of heaven!

I thank You, Lord, for opportunities to lift
my voice in thanksgiving and unite with
other voices that are also praising You.

Living Our Faith

You know your way around the faith.
Now do what you've been taught. School's out;
quit studying the subject and start living it!
And let your living spill over into thanksgiving.
COLOSSIANS 2:7 MSG

Here it is again: the Bible is telling us that thanksgiving is essential to following Jesus. If we want to practice what we preach—or practice what has been preached to us—then it's time for us to start living our faith, allowing our beliefs to become visible in the way we interact with the world around us. Doing that should just naturally spill over into gratitude to God for all He does for us. Believing, living, and thanking become an ongoing cycle that will bless not only our own hearts and lives but everyone whose lives we touch. Thanksgiving is like the body's circulation system, necessary for the ongoing life of our spirits.

Lord, I want to walk the talk, and I want
gratitude to flow through me, carrying
Your Spirit to each aspect of my life.

God Cares for You

*"Consider how the wild flowers grow. They do not labor
or spin. . . . If that is how God clothes the grass of the field,
which is here today, and tomorrow is thrown into the fire,
how much more will he clothe you, you of little faith!"*

LUKE 12:27–28 NIV

If God makes each flower unique and beautiful and sends rain
and sun to meet their needs, will He not also care for you? He
made you. What the Father makes, He loves. And that which
He loves, He cares for. We were made in His image. Humans
are dearer to God than any of His other creations. Rest in Him.
Trust Him. Just as He cares for the birds of the air and the flowers
of the meadows, God will take care of His sons and daughters.
Let Him take care of you.

Father, I am amazed by Your creation.
Remind me that I am Your treasured child.
Take care of me as only You can do. Amen.

Setting Priorities

*Cause me to hear Your lovingkindness in the morning,
for in You do I trust; cause me to know the way in
which I should walk, for I lift up my soul to You.*
Psalm 143:8 nkjv

Twenty-four hours. That's what we get in a day. Though we often think we don't have time for all we want to do, our Creator deemed twenty-four-hour days sufficient. How do we decide what to devote ourselves to? The wisdom of the psalmist tells us to begin the day by asking to hear the loving voice of the one who made us. We can lay our choices, problems, and conflicts before Him in prayer. He will show us which way to go. Hold up that full plate of your life to Him, and allow Him to decide what to keep and what to let go.

Lord, make me willing to surrender my
choices and activities to You. Cause me to
desire the things You want me to do.

Spirit-Oxygen

*Tell me this one thing: How did you receive the
Holy Spirit? Did you receive the Spirit by following
the law? No, you received the Spirit because
you heard the Good News and believed it.*

GALATIANS 3:2 NCV

As we share the good news of Christ, we need to be careful that
we are not preaching the law rather than the love of Christ. The
Spirit did not come into your heart through legalism and laws,
and He won't reach others through you if that is your focus.
Breathe deeply of grace, and let it spread from you to a world
desperate for the oxygen of the Spirit.

Father, Son, and Holy Spirit, how grateful
I am for the good news of the gospel.
Remind me of the grace I have received, and
enable me to share it freely with others. Amen.

God's Name

We give thanks to You, God,
we give thanks, for Your name is near.
PSALM 75:1 NASB

Sometimes we feel as though God is far away. He doesn't seem to have much to do with the details of our daily lives; He seems distant from the chaos of world affairs. This verse from Psalms reminds us that God's name is as close to us as our own. It is always there, available for us to call on. All we need to do is call out God's name, and He will answer us. Maybe not always in the way we expect or hope, but nevertheless, God reveals His presence to us in His answers to prayer. We can give thanks even while we're still praying, as we cry out His name, because we can be confident that He will answer.

———————

I'm calling out Your name, Lord God.
Thank You that You hear me.

Thanksgiving in the Lions' Den

When Daniel learned that the document had been signed, he went into his house. The windows in its upper room opened toward Jerusalem, and three times a day he got down on his knees, prayed, and gave thanks to his God, just as he had done before.

DANIEL 6:10 HCSB

A law had been passed forbidding the people to pray to anyone but King Darius. It meant trouble for Daniel, but he continued to pray to God just as he always had. Even though his life was now in danger, he still gave thanks to God. He knew that God was King of the entire universe; no matter what happened, he trusted God to make things right. Daniel ended up in the lions' den, but the lions didn't eat him. His God protected him.

Lord, when I find myself in a "lions' den" of trouble, help me to trust You as Daniel did; help me to thank You for the work You will do even in my time of danger.

Wrapped in Grace

For the LORD God is a sun and shield:
the LORD will give grace and glory: no good thing
will he withhold from them that walk uprightly.
PSALM 84:11 KJV

When a gift is wrapped in grace, it comes with no strings attached. That's the kind of gift God gives. He doesn't hold eternal life just out of reach, taunting, "If you try harder, this can be yours." He doesn't promise to love us if we never mess up again. He doesn't say He'll forgive but refuse to forget. God graces us with gifts we don't deserve, because His love is deeper than our hearts and minds can comprehend.

I cannot comprehend the depths of Your grace
and love, Lord. I trust that You do not hold my
past against me. Your forgiveness is eternal.
Thank You for wrapping me in grace.

Sharing Life

But if we walk in the light, God himself being the light,
we also experience a shared life with one another.
1 John 1:7 MSG

Some of us are extroverts, and some introverts. But either way, God asks us to share our lives in some way with others. As we walk in His light, He gives us grace to experience a new kind of a life, a life we have in common with the others who share His kingdom.

Lord Jesus, I recognize that You have asked me to share my life with others. Help me to look for opportunities to make connections as I walk in Your light. Amen.

All Humanity

*Let them give thanks to the LORD for His faithful love
and His wonderful works for all humanity. For He has
satisfied the thirsty and filled the hungry with good things.*
PSALM 107:8–9 HCSB

Sometimes we forget how immense the earth is and how many different kinds of people live around the globe. The problems and suffering of those who live on another continent may not seem very real to us, but God does not forget any human being. Each one is real and treasured. He faithfully loves all humanity, and He blesses each person in the way they most need. We can try to catch a glimpse from the divine perspective and perceive all of our planet's inhabitants as one united family, despite our differences. When we do, may our hearts spill over with gratitude for all the ways that God finds to bless the human race.

———

Widen my perspective, Lord, so that I may
experience the love You have for all humanity.

Blessing God

*Bless the LORD, my soul, and do not
forget any of His benefits.*
PSALM 103:2 NASB

At first glance, this verse may seem a little odd. Why would God
need *us* to bless *Him?* Shouldn't it be the other way around? The
original Hebrew word used here, though, meant "to kneel down,
to thank, to praise." This is how we bless God—by surrendering
ourselves to Him, thanking Him, and praising Him. We stop
overlooking all He has done for us, and we offer our gratitude
for each of the blessings (the benefits) He has bestowed on us,
even the small, everyday ones. When we do this, we create a cycle
of blessing that flows from our hearts to God's and back again.

I want to bless You, Lord, as You have so richly
blessed me, so I'm coming to You, thanking
You for all You have done for me.

Why Not Me?

God gave Paul the power to perform unusual miracles.
When handkerchiefs or aprons that had merely touched
his skin were placed on sick people, they were healed.
ACTS 19:11–12 NLT

When his fellow missionary, Trophimus, fell sick, Paul was given no miracle to help him. When Timothy complained of frequent stomach problems, Paul had no miracle-working handkerchief for Timothy's misery. Paul himself suffered from an incurable ailment (2 Corinthians 12:7), yet he was willing to leave it with God. We too may be clueless as to why God miraculously heals some and not others. Like Paul, we must trust God when there's no miracle. Can we be as resilient as Job, who said, "Though he slay me, yet will I trust in him" (Job 13:15 KJV)? We can—waiting for the day when health problems and bad accidents and death cease forever (Revelation 21:4).

———

When healing doesn't come, Lord Jesus, give me
grace to trust You more. Still I choose hope. Amen.

Be Still

*Thou wilt keep him in perfect peace, whose mind
is stayed on thee: because he trusteth in thee.*

ISAIAH 26:3 KJV

Longing for His children to know His peace, God sent prophets like Isaiah to stir up faith, repentance, and comfort in the hearts of the "chosen people." God's message is just as applicable today as it was back then. By keeping our minds fixed on Him, we can have perfect, abiding peace even in the midst of a crazy world. The path to peace is not easy, but it is simple: focus on God. As we meditate on His promises and His faithfulness, He gets bigger, while our problems get smaller.

God, when I focus on the world, my mind and heart feel anxious. Help me to keep my mind on You, so that I can have hope and peace.

An All-the-Time Thing!

Pray diligently. Stay alert,
with your eyes wide open in gratitude.
COLOSSIANS 4:2 MSG

Prayer is not a sometimes thing. It's an all-the-time thing! We need to pray every day, being careful to keep the lines of communication open between God and ourselves all through the day, moment by moment. When we make prayer a habit, we won't miss the many gifts of grace that come our way, and we won't forget to notice when God answers our prayers.

Father, although it's important to set aside specific time for prayer, I am reminded of the value of being in constant communication with You—my good Father, my companion. Amen.

Great Things and Small

The Lord has done great things for us; we are joyful.
PSALM 126:3 NASB

What makes you happy? It might be a sunny day after a week of clouds. It could be good news from a loved one. It might be something as small as a new outfit, a good hair day, or the way a friend makes you laugh. Whatever it is, big or small, God wants us to share it with Him. He doesn't want us to keep our happiness to ourselves. He wants us to remember that everything comes from His hand. The Lord has done great things for us, and He has done countless small things as well. His love is strewn through our lives. As we learn to practice gratitude, our hearts will fill with gladness, and the gladness can then fuel our gratitude, a continual cycle of joy and thanksgiving.

Thank You, Lord, for all You give to
me, for blessings big and small.

Competition and Envy

*Isn't everything you have and everything you
are sheer gifts from God? So what's the point
of all this comparing and competing?*
1 CORINTHIANS 4:7 MSG

Do you ever find yourself comparing your life to others' lives?
Maybe you wonder why a colleague got a raise or a promotion
when you didn't. Or you wish your body was as thin and fit as
your friend's. Envy can be a small twinge that jabs at our contentment, or it can grow into an all-consuming jealousy that saps
the joy from our lives. Either way, it interferes with our practice
of gratitude. Envy and jealousy and competition say, in effect,
that what God has given me isn't *enough*. But God always gives
us exactly what we need. We don't need to compare ourselves to
others because He treats us each as individuals, giving us exactly
what is best.

Lord, may I trust You enough, may my
gratitude be so great, that there's no room
in my life for competition and envy.

Fences

> *"If you keep My commandments, you will abide in My love, just as I have kept My Father's commandments and abide in His love."*
> JOHN 15:10 NKJV

God's commandments are much like the pasture fence. Sin is on the other side. His laws exist to keep us in fellowship with Him and to keep us out of things that are harmful to us that can lead to bondage. We abide in the loving presence of our heavenly Father by staying within the boundaries He has set up for our own good. He has promised to care for us and to do the things needful for us. His love for us is unconditional, even when we jump the fence into sin. But by staying inside the boundaries, we enjoy intimacy with Him.

Father, help me to obey Your commandments that are given for my good. Thank You for Your love for me.

Christ Is Risen Today!

"He isn't here! He is risen from the dead!"
LUKE 24:6 NLT

The power God used to raise Christ from the dead is the same power we have available to us each day to live according to God's will here on earth. What happened on Easter gives us hope for today and for all eternity. If you haven't accepted Jesus Christ as your personal Savior, take the time right now and start your new life in Christ.

Dear Jesus, thank You for dying on the cross for me and taking away all my sin. You are alive and well, and I praise You today for all You are and all You have done. Amen.

A Quiet Pace

"Teach me, and I will be quiet.
Show me where I have been wrong."
JOB 6:24 NCV

Do you ever feel as though you simply can't sit still? That your thoughts are swirling so fast that you can't stop them? That you're so busy, so stressed, so hurried that you have to run, run, run? Take a breath. Open your heart to God. Allow Him to quiet your frantic mind. Ask Him to show you how you can begin again, this time walking to the quiet pace of His grace.

Father, quietness does not always come easily. The frenetic pace of this world sucks me in. Fill my lungs with Your breath. Quiet me and help me to be still. Amen.

Vantage Point

*I will instruct thee and teach thee in the way which
thou shalt go: I will guide thee with mine eye.*
PSALM 32:8 KJV

If you're on a safari, a knowledgeable guide will lead you to the best vantage point to see wildlife, educate you on what you're seeing, and protect you from danger. God is like a safari guide who never leaves your side. He knows both the joys and the dangers that surround you. Through His Spirit and scripture, God will guide you toward a life of wonder and adventure. Stay close to His side and allow Him to lead.

I accept You as my heavenly guide, Holy Spirit.
I want more of You in my life. You are my counselor
and my teacher. I commit to follow where You lead.

Cultivating Thankfulness

*Let the peace of Christ keep you in tune with each other,
in step with each other. None of this going off and doing
your own thing. And cultivate thankfulness. Let the Word
of Christ—the Message—have the run of the house.*
COLOSSIANS 3:15–16 MSG

Yet again the Bible is pointing out how important gratitude is
as a spiritual practice. The implication here is that thankfulness
will act as a bond to keep us in step with others (rather than
arguing and being in competition). Gratitude opens the doors
of our hearts to each other and to Christ as well. It makes space
in us for the Word to have the say in our inner beings as well as
our entire lives. This verse also says that we have control over
how much gratitude is in our lives. We can "cultivate" it, actively
planting the seeds of thanksgiving and constantly watering them
until they grow.

———————————

Teach me, Lord Jesus, to cultivate thankfulness
as my constant spiritual practice.

Humble Gratitude

*Do nothing from selfishness or empty conceit,
but with humility consider one another as more
important than yourselves; do not merely look out for
your own personal interests, but also for the interests
of others. Have this attitude in yourselves which was
also in Christ Jesus, who, as He already existed in
the form of God, did not cosnider equality with God
something to be grasped, but emptied Himself.*

PHILIPPIANS 2:3–7 NASB

Gratitude and pride don't walk together. Pride says, "I don't need to say thank you for anything." It says, "I worry about myself first and foremost." Pride separates us from others. It builds walls. Gratitude, on the other hand, says, "I owe everything to God." It looks for opportunities to say thank you both to God and to others. It draws us closer to one another and to the Lord. It makes us more like Jesus.

Jesus, I want to be like You.
May gratitude drive pride out of my heart.

Praying with Confidence

For we do not have a high priest who is unable to empathize with our weaknesses, but we have one who has been tempted in every way, just as we are— yet he did not sin. Let us then approach God's throne of grace with confidence, so that we may receive mercy and find grace to help us in our time of need.

HEBREWS 4:15–16 NIV

However you're struggling, help is available through Jesus. Our Savior walked on this earth for thirty-three years. He was fully God *and* fully man. He felt hunger. He knew weakness. He was tempted. He felt tired. He "gets it." Go boldly before the throne of grace as a daughter of God. Pray in Jesus' name for an outpouring of His grace and mercy in your life.

Father, I ask You boldly in the name of Christ to help me. My hope is in You alone. Amen.

He Has Chosen You

*Therefore, as God's chosen people, holy and
dearly loved, clothe yourselves with compassion,
kindness, humility, gentleness and patience.*
COLOSSIANS 3:12 NIV

No matter how athletic, beautiful, popular, or smart you are,
you've probably experienced a time when you were chosen last or
overlooked entirely. Being left out is a big disappointment of life
on earth. The good news is that this disappointment isn't part of
God's kingdom. Even when others forget about us, God doesn't.
He has handpicked His beloved children now and forever. The
truth is that Jesus died for *everyone*—every man, woman, and
child who has ever and will ever live. The Father chooses us all.
All we have to do is grab a glove and join the team.

Father, thanks for choosing me. I don't deserve it,
but You call me Your beloved child. Help me to
remember others who may feel overlooked or unloved.
Let Your love for them shine through me. Amen.

Because of Christ

*All this comes from the God who settled the
relationship between us and him, and then called
us to settle our relationships with each other.*
2 CORINTHIANS 5:18 MSG

God created a bridge to span the distance between ourselves
and Him. That bridge is Christ, the best and fullest expression
of divine grace. Because of Christ, we are in a relationship with
the Creator of the entire world. And because of Christ, we are
called to build bridges of our own, to span the distance between
ourselves and others.

Jesus, there is no way I could bridge the
chasm between God and myself. Your sacrifice
draws me near to the Father. May my life
be a reflection of my gratitude. Amen.

From the Inside Out

Take on an entirely new way of life—
a God-fashioned life, a life renewed from the
inside and working itself into your conduct as
God accurately reproduces his character in you.
EPHESIANS 4:24 MSG

At the end of a long week, we sometimes feel tired and drained. We need to use feelings like that as wake-up calls, reminders that we need to open ourselves anew to God's Spirit so that He can renew us from the inside out. Grace has the power to change our hearts and minds, filling us with new energy to follow Jesus.

Lord, the world says change comes from the outside. Your Word says that true transformation comes from the inside. Meet me there—on the inside—and make me like You. Amen.

Unconditional Love

God setteth the solitary in families.
PSALM 68:6 KJV

Family can be one of our greatest joys in this life. It can also be messy because it's where we show our true colors. It's where we're real. That's why "family" is the perfect petri dish for us to learn how to love like Jesus. Unconditional love sees others for who they really are, warts and all, and continues to reach out, sacrifice, and forgive. As we allow God to love us, He will help us more readily love others.

Lord, I cannot truly love others without Your Spirit at work in me. Show me how to love like You do. Infuse me with Your power so I can do it.

Better Acquainted

I will bless the LORD, who hath given me counsel:
my reins also instruct me in the night seasons.
PSALM 16:7 KJV

Suppose you learn CPR in a first-aid class. Years later, when a child nearly drowns at a neighborhood pool, you spring into action. You know exactly what to do. The same is true with the Bible. The better acquainted you become with God's words, the more readily they come to mind when you need them most. When you're unsure of which way to turn, turn to the Bible. It will lead you where you ultimately want to go.

Father, please give me a deep desire for
Your Word. I want to spend time with You,
learning Your truth and knowing You more.

Grace-Full

*For by grace you have been saved through faith;
and this is not of yourselves, it is the gift of God;
not a result of works, so that no one may boast.*
EPHESIANS 2:8–9 NASB

The original Greek word that our Bibles translate as "grace" included gratitude within its meaning. It meant not only that God has freely granted to us His love and blessings, but also that as a result of God's grace, we become "grace-full," which in the original language meant "thankful, grateful." It's one of those reciprocal cycles that are so common in God's kingdom: first God grants us His grace; then we respond with gratitude, which makes us even more full of grace; and then God continues to pour out His grace on us as we continue to respond with thanksgiving.

Lord, may I become ever more
full of grace and gratitude.

Serving God

If by grace, then is it no more of works:
otherwise grace is no more grace. But if it
be of works, then it is no more grace.

ROMANS 11:6 KJV

God calls us to serve Him by carrying out actions of love for others, by giving what we have to those who have less, and by working to build His kingdom here on earth. But we never earn God's love by performing acts of justice and kindness, for God's love is already ours, unconditionally. That is what grace is, and that is why we give all our thanks to God. If we had earned His love and blessings by working hard, we wouldn't need to feel grateful; but since God gives to us freely, regardless of our actions, our hearts overflow with gratitude.

———————

Because I am so grateful for Your freely
given grace, Lord, I want to serve You.

Pride

He gives grace generously. As the Scriptures say,
"God opposes the proud but gives grace to the humble."
JAMES 4:6 NLT

Grace is what God gives us, and gratitude is what we give back to God. Gratitude makes more room in our lives for God's grace, and God's grace makes us ever more grateful. Pride, however, blocks this circular flow that would otherwise proceed naturally from God's heart to ours. Humility, grace, and gratitude accompany one another, but arrogance—the kind of pride that says, "I'm better than everyone else"—interferes with God's generosity. Pride says, "I already have everything I need," and, as a result, no room is left for God's gifts. Humility, however, leads to gratitude, which leads to grace!

Show me, Lord, when I am full of destructive pride.
I don't want to block the flow of Your grace.

The Breath of God

Every part of Scripture is God-breathed and useful one way or another—showing us truth, exposing our rebellion, correcting our mistakes, training us to live God's way.
2 TIMOTHY 3:16 MSG

Do you spend time in God's Word each day? Do you let the breath of God wash over you and comfort you? Are you allowing His Word to penetrate your heart and show you where you've been wrong? If not, you are missing out on one of the most important ways that God chooses to communicate with us today. Ask the Lord for the desire to spend more time in His Word. Don't feel you have the time? Consider using a Bible app, and listen to God's Word as you drive to work or school.

Father, Your Word is so important to me.
Please give me the desire to spend more
time in the Bible each day. Amen.

True Lineage

For thou, O God, hast heard my vows: thou hast given me the heritage of those that fear thy name.
PSALM 61:5 KJV

Your true lineage extends far beyond the branches on your family tree. That's because you have a spiritual heritage as well as a physical one. Your family line extends back through Old and New Testament times, around the world, and right up into today. You may know some of your brothers and sisters by name. Others you may not meet until you walk the streets of heaven together. But God's children are family, linked by faith and a forever future.

Thank You for the family of God You have given me, Father. Please continue to bring people into my life who help draw me closer to You.

Abiding Peace

He himself is our peace.
EPHESIANS 2:14 NIV

Regardless of life's circumstances, hope and peace are available if Jesus is there. You do not have to succumb to getting buffeted and beaten by the storms of life. Seek refuge in the center of the storm. Run to the arms of Jesus, the Prince of Peace. Let Him wipe your tears and calm your fears. Like the eye of the hurricane, His presence brings peace and calm. Move yourself closer. Desire to be in His presence for He is your peace. As you abide in His presence, peace will envelop you. The raging around you may not subside, but the churning of your heart will. You will find rest for your soul.

Dear Lord, thank You for being our peace in the midst of life's fiercest storms. Amen.

Our Abundant God

We have all received grace after grace from His fullness.
JOHN 1:16 HCSB

Our God is not a stingy God, nor does He lack resources from which to draw. No, God is full, abundant, overflowing, and He shares all that He is with limitless generosity. We have so many reasons to be grateful, for He has given us "grace after grace." He blesses us daily with physical blessings; but even more, He piles spiritual blessings onto our souls. When we have eyes to see, we realize that everywhere we turn, God is there, blessing us, pouring out His generous grace in more ways than we could possibly imagine.

Thank You, Lord, that You are such an abundant God!

A Thousand Generations

"GOD, a God of mercy and grace, endlessly patient—
so much love, so deeply true—loyal in love for a thousand
generations, forgiving iniquity, rebellion, and sin."
EXODUS 34:6 MSG

What an amazing God we have. This verse seems to say it all: God is full of mercy and kindness; He doesn't treat us the way we "deserve" but instead is endlessly patient with our mistakes and failures. His love is so deep, so loyal, so true, that it stretches back a thousand generations. Long, long ago, God was already loving us, already planning to bless us, already forgiving us for our rebellion against Him, already planning to heal us and make us whole. No wonder our hearts spill over with gratitude!

I can't begin to grasp Your love, Lord.
It fills me with awe and a deep, deep gratitude
that goes down to the roots of my being.

Focus Time

In the morning, LORD, you hear my voice; in the morning
I lay my requests before you and wait expectantly.
PSALM 5:3 NIV

What is the first thing you do each morning? Many of us hit
the ground running, armed with to-do lists a mile long. While it
doesn't ensure perfection, setting aside a short time each morning
to focus on the Father and the day ahead can help prepare us to
live more intentionally. During this time we, like Jesus, gain clarity
so that we can invest our lives in the things that truly matter.

———————

Father, help me to take time each morning to focus
on You and the day ahead. Align my priorities so that
the things I do will be the things You want me to do.

The Missing Pieces

Trust the LORD with all your heart,
and don't depend on your own understanding.
PROVERBS 3:5 NCV

Life is confusing. No matter how hard we try, we can't always make sense of it. We don't like it when that happens, and so we keep trying to determine what's going on, as though we were trying puzzle pieces to fill in a picture we long to see. Sometimes, though, we have to accept that in this life we will never be able to see the entire image. We have to trust God's grace for the missing pieces.

Dear Lord, my own understanding is very limited, and yet I still sometimes try to depend on it. Help me to trust You with 100 percent of my heart. Amen.

Glimpses of God

Glory ye in his holy name: let the heart of them
rejoice that seek the LORD. Seek the LORD,
and his strength: seek his face evermore.
PSALM 105:3–4 KJV

Babies often smile when they catch sight of their mother's face.
Catching a glimpse of God can do the same for us. It can make
our hearts happy. Yet God's presence is much more subtle than
that of a human parent. God reveals Himself in quiet ways,
such as in an answer to prayer, the glory of a sunset, or the gift
of a new friend. Keep your eyes open. God is ever present and
at work in your life.

Father, I want to see You at work in my life.
Open my spiritual eyes to see You. Thank You in
advance for answering my prayers in this way.

Polarization

*That you may learn from us. . .that none of you will be
inflated with pride in favor of one person over another.*
1 Corinthians 4:6 HCSB

When Paul wrote this to the church at Corinth, the people there
were having a problem with partisanship. Some of them followed
Paul; others followed Peter. That would have been fine if both
groups had respected each other, but instead they became rivals.
The community was polarized between Paul followers and Peter
followers. The situation was actually a lot like what we face in
our country today, where so many people have allowed politics to
become a source of pride and division. "Learn from both of us,"
Paul says. "Be humble. Make room for others' opinions and treat
them with respect. Stop being so full of certainty that you're the
only one who's right. Create space for humility and gratitude."

I thank You, God, that You understand our
complicated world. May gratitude and humility open
my heart to those who think differently than me.

True

"God's grace and truth go with you!"
2 Samuel 15:20 MSG

We are grateful for God's grace, but why do we need His truth? What is the Bible saying here? Maybe we need God's truth because in a world where so much is false, we can count on God to always be real. Other versions of the Bible translate "truth" as "faithfulness," and the original Hebrew word used here meant "reliability, steadiness, certainty, continuity," as well as "true." Think about it: Lies don't last; sooner or later they are exposed. Lies can't be depended on; sooner or later they let us down. Lies are shaky ground on which to build our lives. We can be grateful that our God is reliable, steady, faithful—and true.

Lord, I thank You that You are the truth at the center of my life, the steady rock under my feet.

Confidence

*For I know that my redeemer liveth, and that
he shall stand at the latter day upon the earth:
and though after my skin worms destroy this
body, yet in my flesh shall I see God.*

JOB 19:25–26 KJV

Although we experience various difficulties throughout life, we can still look forward to the blessed future we have. No matter what our struggles are, our Lord controls. Job had no idea what the purpose of his trial was, but he faced his troubles with confidence, knowing that ultimately he would emerge victorious. Too many times we view our own situations with self-pity rather than considering God's strength and trusting that His plan is perfect. What peace God offers when we finally cast our cares on Him and with great conviction declare, "I know that my redeemer liveth!"

Oh great Redeemer, in You I have confidence
even when I don't understand life's trials.
Please help me to live victoriously.

The Perfect Reflection

"Give careful thought to your ways."
HAGGAI 1:7 NIV

As we give careful thought to our ways, we should first look back to where we have come from and reflect on God's work in our lives. We are on a journey. Sometimes the road is difficult; sometimes the road is easy. We must consider where we were when God found us and where we are now through His grace. Even more importantly, we must think about the ways our present actions, habits, and attitude toward God reflect our lives as Christians. Only when we are able to honestly assess our lives in Christ can we call on His name to help perfect our reflection.

Dear Lord, help me to look honestly at the ways I live and make changes where necessary. Amen.

His Healing Abundance

"Behold, I will bring it health and healing;
I will heal them and reveal to them the
abundance of peace and truth."
JEREMIAH 33:6 NKJV

If we confess our sins to God, He will bring relief to our souls. When we're distressed, we have Jesus, the prince of peace, to give us peace. When our emotions threaten to overwhelm us, we can implore Jehovah-Rapha—the God who heals—to calm our anxious hearts. When we're physically sick, we can cry out to Jesus, our great physician. Whether our problems affect us physically, spiritually, mentally, or emotionally, we can trust that God will come to us and bring us healing. And beyond our temporal lives, we can look forward with hope to our heavenly lives. There we will be healthy, whole, and alive—forever.

Jehovah-Rapha, thank You for healing me. Help me do my part to seek health and the abundance of peace and truth You provide.

First Priorities

For Wisdom is better than all the trappings of wealth;
nothing you could wish for holds a candle to her.
PROVERBS 8:11 MSG

What do you value most? You may know the answer you are
"supposed" to give to that question, but you can tell the real answer
by where your time and energy are focused. Do you spend most
of your time working for and thinking about money and physical
wealth, or do you make wisdom and grace your first priorities?

Father, if I compare myself too much with
others, I can easily get caught in the trappings
of wealth. Instead, turn my focus to You, and
help me to make wisdom my goal. Amen.

Sheer Generosity

*Out of sheer generosity he put us in right standing
with himself. A pure gift. He got us out of the mess
we're in and restored us to where he always wanted
us to be. And he did it by means of Jesus Christ.*
ROMANS 3:24 MSG

We are grateful when someone gives us a birthday or Christmas
gift, but we are even more thankful when someone surprises us
with a present out of the blue for no particular occasion or reason.
That's sheer generosity, with no sense of obligation involved. Jesus
is God's gift to us, a gift He didn't have to give, that He was under
no obligation to offer, and yet He did. Through Jesus, we find
ourselves lifted out of our failures and mistakes. Through this
most amazing of gifts, we are drawn close to God and wrapped
in His love. How can we respond to such generosity except with
hearts full of gratitude?

Thank You, Jesus, for the gift of Yourself.

Overflowing Grace

*God is able to make every grace overflow to you,
so that in every way, always having everything
you need, you may excel in every good work.*
2 CORINTHIANS 9:8 HCSB

Do you ever feel as though you don't have enough of what you need? Maybe you don't think you have enough money, or maybe you don't believe you're talented enough or intelligent enough to do a job that you've been given. When you have those feelings of inadequacy, turn them into gratitude, for God has promised to give you not only everything you need but even *more* than you need, so that you can excel in the work of His kingdom.

Thank You, Jesus, that Your grace overflows.

Always Thinking of You

What is man that You are mindful of him,
and the son of man that You visit him?
PSALM 8:4 NKJV

Have you ever wondered what God thinks about? *You* are always on His mind. In all you think and do, He considers you and makes intercession for you. He knows the thoughts and intents of your heart. He understands you like no other person can. He knows your strengths and weaknesses, your darkest fears and highest hopes. He's constantly aware of your feelings and how you interact with or without Him each day. God is always with you, waiting for you to remember Him—to call on Him for help, for friendship, for anything you need.

Lord, help me to remember You as I go throughout
my day. I want to include You in my life and
always be thinking of You too. Amen.

Control

Put GOD in charge of your work,
then what you've planned will take place.
PROVERBS 16:3 MSG

If we're doing a job that is important to us, it is hard to let go of our control. Not only do we hate to trust someone else to take over, but we often don't want to trust God to take charge either. We want to do it all by ourselves. But the best laid plans fall into nothing without God's help. What's more, as we rely on His grace, we no longer need to feel stressed or pressured! We can let Him take charge.

God, the more I entrust my plans to You, the more successful they will be. Give me the courage to trust and the grace to rest in Your promise. Amen.

Nurturing a Happy Heart

*Because thou hast been my help, therefore in
the shadow of thy wings will I rejoice.*
PSALM 63:7 KJV

Happiness can be contagious. Why not spread some of yours
around? Consider the ways God helps you nurture a happy heart.
How has He comforted you, encouraged you, strengthened you?
If you're happy, share it. Tell someone close to you what God
has done. Smile warmly at those who cross your path. Surprise
someone with a gift just because. Express to God how you feel
in song. Thank God for the little things—such as the ability to
feel happy.

Father, will You fill my heart with contagious
joy? I want to spread Your love to those
who need it most. Help me to show deep,
authentic love to those around me.

Growing in Grace

Grow in grace, and in the knowledge of
our Lord and Saviour Jesus Christ.
2 PETER 3:18 KJV

If grace is a gift from God, how does it make sense that we can *grow in grace*? What did the apostle Peter mean when he wrote these words? Perhaps he understood that gratitude is the other side of grace, and the more gratitude we feel toward God, the more we open ourselves to greater grace. Peter gives us a clue to what he means in this verse. He indicates that as we get to know Jesus better, we will also grow in grace. Gratitude opens our hearts to a deeper relationship with Jesus, and grace pours out from the relationship. This is the way we grow spiritually; this is the way we grow into the people God created us to be.

I want to get to know You better, Jesus.
I am so grateful for all You have done for me.

Pour Out Prayers

*Trust in Him at all times, you people; pour out
your heart before Him; God is a refuge for us.*
PSALM 62:8 NKJV

The psalmist tells us to trust the Lord at all times and to pour
out our hearts to Him. There is nothing we think or feel that
He does not already know. He longs for us to come to Him,
spilling out our thoughts, needs, and desires. God invites us to
an open-ended conversation. He made us for relationship with
Him. He never tires of listening to His children. The Lord is our
helper. He is our refuge. He knows the solutions to our problems
and the wisdom we need for living each day.

Lord, remind me of Your invitation to pour out my
problems to You. You are my refuge and my helper.
Help me to trust You with every detail of my life.

Lasting Treasure

"Beware! Guard against every kind of greed.
Life is not measured by how much you own."
LUKE 12:15 NLT

The Lord never meant for us to be satisfied with temporary treasures. Earthly possessions leave us empty because our hearts are fickle. Once we gain possession of one thing, our hearts yearn for something else. Lasting treasure can only be found in Jesus Christ. He brings contentment so that the treasure chests of our souls overflow in abundance. Hope is placed in the Lord rather than our net-worth statement. Joy is received by walking with the Lord, not by chasing some fleeting fancy. Love is showered upon us as we grab hold of real life, life that cannot be bought but that can only be given through Jesus Christ.

Dear Lord, may I be content with what You have given me. May I not wish for more material treasures but seek eternal wealth from You. Amen.

I Lift My Eyes

I lift up my eyes to the mountains—where does my help come from? My help comes from the LORD, the Maker of heaven and earth.
PSALM 121:1–2 NIV

Adulthood is a time when decisions can be the most crucial. Challenges, failures, doubts, and fears may cloud decisions and cripple us into inaction because the end result is unknown. Career paths, relationships, and financial decisions are only some of the areas that cause concern. In all of those things and in all of life, we shouldn't keep our heads down and simply plow through. Instead, we must lift our eyes to the Lord. If we fix our focus on Jesus, we will see that He is prepared to lead and guide us through all of life's challenges.

Lord, I lift my eyes to You. Please guide me down the path of life. Let me never become so focused on my own goals or so busy that I forget to look to You, for You are my help. Amen.

Strong, Firm, and Steadfast

The God of all grace, who called you to his eternal glory in Christ, after you have suffered a little while, will himself restore you and make you strong, firm and steadfast.
1 PETER 5:10 NIV

Following Jesus doesn't mean we never experience hard times. The Bible is clear about this. And no matter how spiritually mature we are, we will always encounter times of doubt and suffering. But even in the midst of those painful times, we can still be grateful. The God of grace—the God who gives to us so freely and unconditionally—will never abandon us to the hard moments of our lives. He won't leave us there. In His good time, He will reach down and restore us, healing our doubts and comforting our pain so that we are once again strong, firm, and steadfast.

Remind me, Lord, to be grateful in the hard times, confident that You will rescue me.

Bitter Roots

See to it that no one comes short of the grace of God;
that no root of bitterness springing up causes trouble.
HEBREWS 12:15 NASB

God's grace is unconditional, but we have the power to cut ourselves off from it. This verse speaks of a "root of bitterness" that can cause us to "come short" of God's grace. In Greek, the word our Bibles have translated as "come short" meant "to come late, causing a lack." God is pouring out His grace, but we fail to show up on time to receive it. As a result, we don't have everything we need because we let bitterness (resentment, jealousy, and hatred) take root in our hearts. How do we pull out that root? With gratitude. Turning to God with a thankful heart leaves no more room for bitterness to grow.

I ask You, Lord, to pull out by the roots any bitterness growing in my heart. May my gratitude for all You have done for me make more room for Your grace.

Immense and Incredible

*Immense in mercy and with an incredible love,
he embraced us. He took our sin-dead lives and made
us alive in Christ. He did all this on his own, with no
help from us! Then he picked us up and set us down in
highest heaven in company with Jesus, our Messiah.*

Ephesians 2:4–6 msg

We have so many reasons to feel gratitude. First, God embraced us; the Creator of the universe felt such incredible love for us, such immense mercy, that He reached out to hug us tight. Then, through Christ, He brought back to life everything in us that was dead, and He did it on His own initiative, with no effort on our part. As if that weren't enough, He picked us up and placed us in heaven, with Jesus to keep us company. The next time you have a hard time feeling grateful for much of anything, think about *that*.

Father, thank You for embracing me with
Your all-encompassing love. My heart is
overflowing with gratitude today.

Humble Clothes

All of you clothe yourselves with humility
toward one another, because God resists the
proud but gives grace to the humble.
1 PETER 5:5 HCSB

Once again we have the Bible's formula for spiritual happiness
and growth: humility + gratitude = God's grace. Grace and gratitude reflect one another, and both find their place in our hearts
when we live lives of humility rather than pride. Yet it's so easy
sometimes to interact with others from a place of pride. We fear
being hurt; we worry that people will think we're silly or look
down on us. But the apostle Peter is telling us here that we don't
need to erect a shield of pride around our heart for protection.
Instead, we can clothe ourselves with humility. This is soft and
gentle clothing that allows others to come close to us. It allows
God's grace to soak into our hearts.

Remind me, Jesus, to clothe myself in the
same humility that You wore, and may I
always be humble enough to be grateful.

Christ-Balance

Jesus caught them off balance with his own test question:
"What do you think about the Christ? Whose son is he?"
MATTHEW 22:41–42 MSG

Sometimes Christ asks us to find new ways of thinking. . .new ways of living. . .new ways of encountering Him in the world around us. That is not always easy. We don't like to be caught off balance. When our life's equilibrium is shaken, we feel anxious, out of control. But if we rely on Christ, He will pick us up, dust us off, and give us the grace to find our balance in Him.

Dear Jesus, sometimes I think I have things all figured out, then You ask a hard question. When I am thrown off balance, steady me with Your truth. Amen.

Hope and Healing

My flesh and my heart faileth: but God is the
strength of my heart, and my portion for ever.
PSALM 73:26 KJV

Your body is amazingly resilient yet terminally fragile. Fashioned by God's lovingly creative hand, it was not designed to last. But you were. That's because you are so much more than your body. But God cares about all of you, your body and your soul. Even if your health fails, He will not. He is near. He hears every prayer, even those you hesitate to pray. Call on Him. His hope and healing reach beyond this life into the next.

––––––––––––––

Your Word tells me that You set eternity in my heart when You created me, Lord. Thank You for loving me that much! I can't wait to be with You for all eternity.

True Beauty

What matters is not your outer appearance—
the styling of your hair, the jewelry you wear, the cut of
your clothes—but your inner disposition. Cultivate inner
beauty, the gentle, gracious kind that God delights in.

1 PETER 3:3–4 MSG

We want to be beautiful. It's a longing that has been in our hearts since we were little girls. As grown-up women, we can become overly worried about our appearance, fretting over whether we measure up to the demanding standards of that little girl who still lives in our hearts. We need to relax in the assurance of God's grace within us. As we allow His Spirit to shine through us, we will find our deepest, truest beauty.

God, instead of focusing on the image I see in my mirror, help me to look into Your eyes for an accurate reflection of the beauty You have instilled in me. Amen.

He Is Faithful

If we are unfaithful, he remains faithful,
for he cannot deny who he is.
2 TIMOTHY 2:13 NLT

Sometimes we treat our relationship with God the same as we do with other people. We promise Him we'll spend more time with Him in prayer and Bible study. Soon the daily distractions of life get in the way, and we're back in our same routine, minus prayer and Bible study. Even when we fail to live up to our expectations, our heavenly Father doesn't pick up His judge's gavel and condemn us for unfaithfulness. Instead, He remains a faithful supporter, encouraging us to keep trying to hold up our end of the bargain. Take comfort in His faithfulness, and let that encourage you toward a deeper relationship with Him.

Father, thank You for Your unending faithfulness.
Every day I fall short of Your standards, but
You're always there, encouraging me and lifting
me up. Please help me to be more faithful to You
in the big things and the little things. Amen.

Reason to Be Grateful

*God, who set me apart from my mother's womb and
called me by his grace, was pleased to reveal his Son in me.*
GALATIANS 1:15–16 NIV

Sometimes it's hard to see much reason for gratitude. The troubles
in our lives can loom so large and dark that we have difficulty
perceiving God's grace. In times like that, it's good to reread Bible
verses that remind us of all God has done for us. We were loved
as individuals before we were even born. God has a particular
plan for each one of us. And God reveals Christ to the world
through each of us uniquely. That knowledge is humbling, and
it's good reason to feel grateful, even in the midst of life's darkness
and difficulties.

Thank You, God, for loving me,
for calling me, for using me in Your kingdom.

True Wealth

*Tell those rich in this world's wealth to quit being so full
of themselves and so obsessed with money, which is here
today and gone tomorrow. Tell them to go after God, who
piles on all the riches we could ever manage—to do good,
to be rich in helping others, to be extravagantly generous.*
1 TIMOTHY 6:17–18 MSG

If given material blessings in the form of financial security, we
can feel grateful for God's provision, but we need to remember
that money is only a temporary blessing. It comes and goes, and
we cannot take it with us when we leave this world. These verses
tell us to focus on a different sort of riches: the spiritual wealth of
being able to help others, of being able to give generously. When
we do, we participate in God's free-flowing grace—a form of
wealth that is eternal. And it's good reason to be truly grateful.

Lord, thank You that I have the privilege
of being used by You to bless others.

Trembling While Trusting

*And straightway the father of the
child cried out, and said with tears,
Lord, I believe; help thou mine unbelief.*
MARK 9:24 KJV

When the Lord looks at us, what does He see? Do we trust
Him enough to be vulnerable? Are we willing to obey even when
we are afraid? Do we believe Him? Do not be afraid to follow
Him, and do not let your trembling hold you back. Be willing
to take a step of faith. If you are scared, God understands and
is compassionate and merciful. Fear does not negate His love
for you. Your faith will grow as you trust Him. Let's trust even
while trembling.

———————————

Dear Lord, help my unbelief. Enable me to trust
You even though I may be trembling. Amen.

Sense of Belonging

"All that the Father gives Me will come to Me, and the one who comes to Me I will by no means cast out."
JOHN 6:37 NKJV

We belong to Christ. When the Father calls us to come to Jesus, we belong to Him. This is an irrevocable transaction. We are His, given to Him by the Father. He does not refuse to save us. He will not refuse to help us. No detail of our lives is unimportant to Him. No matter what happens, He will never let us go. Like the enduring love of a parent—but even more perfect—is the love of Christ for us. He has endured all the temptations and suffered all the pain that we will ever face. He has given His very life for us. We can live peacefully and securely knowing we belong to Him.

Jesus, I confess I often forget that I belong to You and how much You love me. Help me to rest in Your everlasting love and care. Amen.

Just What We Need

*God can pour on the blessings in astonishing ways
so that you're ready for anything and everything,
more than just ready to do what needs to be done.*
2 CORINTHIANS 9:8 MSG

Blessings are God's grace visible to us in tangible form. Sometimes they are so small we nearly overlook them—the sun on our faces, the smile of a friend, or food on the table—but other times they amaze us. Day by day, God's grace makes us ready for whatever comes our way. He gives us exactly what we need.

God, the more I see Your blessings, the more they seem to pour out on me. Give me Your grace to receive and eyes to see Your goodness. Amen.

A Gift

Don't you see that children are GOD's best gift?
PSALM 127:3 MSG

Whether we have children of our own or enjoy others' children, God's grace is revealed to us in a special way through these small people. In children, we catch a glimpse of what God intended for us all, before we grew up and let life cloud our hearts. Children's hope gives us grown-ups hope as well. Their laughter makes us smile, and their love reminds us that we too are loved by God.

Father, thank You for the joy that children bring and the beautiful illustration of Your love for us. Thank You for the life lessons little ones have to teach us. Amen.

More Than a Passing Acquaintance

They looked unto him, and were lightened:
and their faces were not ashamed.
PSALM 34:5 KJV

People often ask "How are you?" as a formality. What they want to hear is "Fine!" Nothing more. But God wants more than a passing acquaintance with you. He invites you to share not only what you want and need, but also how you feel. God created you as a woman with complex emotions. You need never hesitate to share your tears with the one who knows you and loves you through and through.

Creator God, You made me beautifully feminine,
and I accept that and join You in Your will for me as
a woman. I ask Your blessing on my life as I seek You.

Sticking Together

Families stick together in all kinds of trouble.
PROVERBS 17:17 MSG

Families can drive you crazy. Whether it's the people with whom you share a house or the extended family that gets together at holidays and birthdays, family members can be exasperating, even infuriating. When it comes right down to it, though, your family members are the ones who show you God's grace even when life is hard, the ones who stick by you no matter what (even when they make you crazy!).

Heavenly Father, thank You for my family.
Thank You for opportunities to give and receive
Your grace. When I am exasperated, remind me
of the patience You have with me. Amen.

Healthy Habits

He healeth the broken in heart,
and bindeth up their wounds.
PSALM 147:3 KJV

Good health is a matter of both prayer and practice. As with every detail of our lives, God wants us to share our health concerns with Him. But God also asks us to take an active role in caring for our bodies. The way we care for a gift reveals what we truly feel about the giver as well as what we've received. Practicing healthy habits is a thank-you note to God for His gift of life.

Father, I pray that You would give me wisdom
to seek healthy habits in my mind, body,
and spirit. I am Your temple. Help me treat
my body in a way that honors You.

Don't Forget!

*Praise the LORD, my soul; all my inmost being,
praise his holy name. Praise the LORD, my soul,
and forget not all his benefits—who forgives all
your sins and heals all your diseases, who redeems
your life from the pit and crowns you with love and
compassion, who satisfies your desires with good
things so that your youth is renewed like the eagle's.*

PSALM 103:1–5 NIV

Our God is endlessly good to us, but the psalmist understood that our souls need to be reminded of everything God does. He forgives our sins; He heals us; He redeems us; He honors us with His love and compassion; He satisfies our hearts' desires; and He renews our spirits so that even in old age they rise up like an eagle's. When our souls remember all these blessings, they brim over with praise and thanks. Gratitude sinks down into our innermost being and then spills over into our entire lives.

I am so grateful, God,
for everything You have done for me.

Undeserved

Christ has brought us into this place of undeserved privilege where we now stand, and we confidently and joyfully look forward to sharing God's glory.

ROMANS 5:2 NLT

Through Christ, we have an intimate relationship with God. The Creator of the universe considers us to be just as much His children as Jesus is. That means that Jesus is our brother. We can look forward to an eternity of sharing God's light and life with Jesus, beginning now and never ending.

We didn't do anything to earn the privilege of being God's children. Christ did it for us simply because He loved us. All we have to do is say, "Thank You."

Father God, I am so grateful to be Your child.

Enjoy Every Minute

One who moves too hurriedly misses the way.
PROVERBS 19:2 NRSV

Hurry. Faster. Accomplish more. Learn this. Study that. Time's wasting. Do more for God. Messages like these fly around us daily, whether they're blatant or inferred. Perhaps you've sensed the rush and have become too busy, trying to do it all. Now you're tired. How can you change? First, know that God isn't the one pressing the HURRY button. He doesn't want you to dash through life and lose your way. He wants you to slow down and enjoy every minute.

———

Father, please change my heart and actions
from striving to do everything that seems good
to seeking Your presence in every moment.

Women Who Loved Well

Charm is deceptive, and beauty is fleeting.
PROVERBS 31:30 NIV

In the end, it will matter to Jesus, of course, that we knew Him as our friend and Savior, but it will also matter that while we walked this earthly life, we loved well. That we saw a need and met it. That we smiled when we wanted to frown. That we were handier with a cup of cool water than a witty comeback. That we chased after a lost soul faster than we chased after a good time. That we loved other people as ourselves. Those things will matter a great deal, and with the power of the Holy Spirit, all those things are within our grasp. They are also ours to give away fully, freely—and daily.

Heavenly Father, help me to focus on cultivating those qualities and virtues that are lasting and will make an eternal impact for Your kingdom. Amen.

Right People—
Right Place—Right Time

And so find favor and high esteem
in the sight of God and man.
PROVERBS 3:4 NKJV

God wants you to experience every favor and rich blessing He's prepared. By faith, expect blessing to meet you at every turn. Imagine what your future holds when you become determined to step out to greet it according to God's design. Remain alert and attentive to what God wants to add to your life. Expect the goodness He has planned for you—doors of opportunities are opening for you today!

Lord, thank You for setting favor and blessing
in my path, and help me to expect it wherever
I go and in whatever I do. Amen.

Sensitivity

*At the same time, don't be callous in your exercise
of freedom, thoughtlessly stepping on the toes
of those who aren't as free as you are. I try my
best to be considerate of everyone's feelings in
all these matters; I hope you will be, too.*
1 CORINTHIANS 10:32–33 MSG

The person who walks in grace doesn't trip over other people's
feet. She doesn't shove her way through life like a bull in a china
shop. Instead, she allows the grace she has so freely received
to make her more aware of others' feelings. With God-given
empathy, she is sensitive to those around her, sharing the grace
she has received with all she meets.

Jesus, I am grateful for the freedom I have in
You. Help me to see past my differences with
others so that I can show them empathy from
a gracious and compassionate heart. Amen.

Gratitude Versus Negativity

*For if by the one man's trespass the many died, how much
more have the grace of God and the gift overflowed to
the many by the grace of the one man, Jesus Christ.*
ROMANS 5:15 HCSB

We live in a world of negativity. The news we hear focuses on tragedies and controversies. The social media posts that come up on our feed often seem geared to incite feelings of anger and despair. The Bible agrees that sin is a very real problem in the world, but scripture is not negative. Yes, sin exists, but the grace of God is so much more abundant than any darkness our world offers. Genesis tells the story of how death and sin entered the world through Adam, but the Gospels tell the story of God's grace through another man, Jesus Christ. Through Him we can turn away from negativity and despair and instead focus on our gratitude for God's overflowing grace.

Thank You, Jesus, that You are the
answer to the world's negativity.

Guilt

Because of his grace he made us right in his sight and
gave us confidence that we will inherit eternal life.
TITUS 3:7 NLT

Carrying around guilt on our shoulders is a terrible feeling. It can lead to depression and fear. It leaves no room for gratitude. But God doesn't want us to live our lives in that state. That's why Jesus came—so that we could know we are right with God. We don't have to feel guilty. We don't have to feel sad or scared. Instead, we can be confident that God has set us free from all our failures and mistakes, and through Jesus, we will live with God forever in eternity. When we focus on that reality, our guilt will slip away, leaving only gratitude for all that God has done for us.

I am so grateful, Jesus, that because of
You, I no longer have to feel guilty.

Finish Line

I have fought the good fight,
I have finished the race, I have kept the faith.
2 TIMOTHY 4:7 NIV

Paul felt his life was coming to an end. As he wrote to his friend Timothy, he spoke of this. He was not boasting, he was just giving his status report, as it were. Good fight fought? Check. Race finished? Check (well, almost). Faith kept? Check. What does your checklist include? What accomplishments make your list? What goals do you want to be known for achieving? What do you want to do, who do you want to become, before your race is finished? Write them down today. Put a checkbox by each one. Then go and work out your life, faith, and ministry for all you're worth. Godspeed.

Dear Lord, bless the work of my hands and
feet. Make me Your servant so that at
the end of my life, I can look forward to
hearing You say, "Well done." Amen.

Experiencing Fellowship

*I will praise thee for ever, because thou
hast done it: and I will wait on thy name;
for it is good before thy saints.*
PSALM 52:9 KJV

Fellowship is a fancy word for getting together with others who love God. It's more than going to church. It's doing life together. Whether you're meeting as a small group for Bible study or simply chatting one-on-one over a cup of coffee about what God is doing in your lives, you're experiencing fellowship. When faith and friendship come together with honesty and authenticity, relationships thrive—between you and God and between you and your spiritual brothers and sisters.

Father, please place God-honoring people in my
life who speak the truth in loving ways. Fill us with
joy as we gather together in Your presence.

The Impossible

*Arise, O Lord; O God, lift up thine
hand: forget not the humble.*
PSALM 10:12 KJV

God spoke the cosmos into being. He fashioned the ebb and flow of the tides. He breathed life into what was once nothing more than dust. This same awesome God is reaching down to offer His help to you today. Perhaps your prayer is for your own needs. Or maybe it's for those you care about but don't know how to help. God is mighty enough and loving enough to do the impossible.

Lord, I believe You can do more than all I could ask
or imagine! I trust that You are the Creator of all
and that You want an intimate relationship with me.

Friends

Two people are better off than one,
for they can help each other succeed.
ECCLESIASTES 4:9 NLT

Our friends are gifts from God. Marcel Proust wrote, "Let us be grateful to the people who make us happy; they are the charming gardeners who make our souls blossom." God comes into our lives through the people we know and love. He uses them to help our souls blossom; with the help of another, we can go further, reach higher, and succeed where we otherwise might have failed. This scripture is a reminder not to take our friends for granted but instead to thank God for them daily, realizing that He uses them to bless us.

———————

Thank You for the people You have put in my life, Lord. I pray that I may bless them as much as they bless me.

Full of Faith and Power

*Stephen, full of faith and power, did great
wonders and miracles among the people.*
ACTS 6:8 KJV

Sometimes we look at other people and feel amazed by all they accomplish. Next to them, we may even feel a bit inadequate. This verse reminds us, though, that God is the one who gives each of us our gifts. Stephen could do such great works because of his faith in God. We can be grateful for the "Stephens" of the world, and at the same time, we can thank God for the unique gifts He has given to each of us. We are not all called to be Stephens, doing amazing acts that draw the attention of people. Some of us may be called to work quietly, behind the scenes, our gifts seldom if ever noticed but no less deserving of gratitude.

Give me the faith and power I need, Lord, to do the work to which You have called me, and help me never to forget to thank You for what You do through me.

Wisdom and Grace

*"Prize [wisdom], and she will exalt you; she
will honor you if you embrace her. She will
place on your head a garland of grace; she
will present you with a crown of beauty."*
PROVERBS 4:8–9 NASB

These verses summarize once again the reciprocal nature of grace
and gratitude. As we honor and embrace wisdom—which the
Old Testament describes as being an aspect of God—and as
we thank God for all wisdom teaches us and gives to us, we are
in return lifted up and crowned, our lives graced with beauty.
Wisdom gives us reason to be grateful, and then our gratitude
leads to still greater grace, a garland of grace that encircles our
entire lives with loveliness, filling our hearts still more with
gratitude for wisdom's gifts. When grace is everywhere we turn,
how can we help but overflow with thankfulness?

Source of wisdom, I honor You and
embrace You; I am so grateful for the
grace You bestow upon my life.

Every Step of the Way

Never stop praying.
1 Thessalonians 5:17 nlt

Several passages in the Bible tell us clearly that God listens to us when we pray. He hears every word and is compassionate. All we have to do is share our concerns with Him and wait faithfully for what He will provide.

God wants to be involved in our daily routines. He wants to hear from us and waits for us. God never promised an easy life to Christians. If we will allow Him, though, God will be there with us every step of the way. All we need to do is come to Him in prayer. With these three simple words from 1 Thessalonians 5:17, our lives can be fulfilling as we live to communicate with our Lord.

Father, when I pray, remind me that prayer is not only about talking to You but also about listening to You. Open my heart to Your words. Amen.

Harm for Good

"You intended to harm me, but God intended it for good."
GENESIS 50:20 NIV

Joseph suffered more in his lifetime than any of us ever will. But God remembered him, blessed him, and made him a man of great authority so that he was in the position to make wise decisions and save many people from starvation.

Instead of feeling entitled to apologies, Joseph wanted redemption in place of revenge. In response to his brothers wanting security, he replied, "Don't be afraid. Am I in the place of God? You intended to harm me, but God intended it for good to accomplish what is now being done, the saving of many lives" (Genesis 50:19–20).

Maybe you're in the middle of suffering right now, so deep in it you can't possibly see any good. Take encouragement from Joseph's words. You are not God—you cannot see what He sees. Maybe yet there will be some good that comes out of the harm.

Dear God, help me to trust in Your plans. Amen.

Open Homes

*Be quick to give a meal to the hungry,
a bed to the homeless—cheerfully.*
1 PETER 4:9 MSG

Because our homes are our private places, the places we retreat to when we're tired to find new strength, it's hard sometimes to open our homes to others. It's bad enough that we have to cope with others' needs all day long, we feel, without having to bring them home with us! But God calls us to offer our hospitality, and He will give us the grace to do it joyfully.

God, You have blessed me with a home—
a sanctuary. And I am so grateful for it. Help me
to joyfully share that blessing with others. Amen.

Freedom

"If the Son sets you free, you really will be free."
JOHN 8:36 HCSB

Many things can keep us from being free. Certain relationships can be so unhealthy that they rob us of our freedom. Addiction—whether to alcohol or drugs or to a particular behavior—can also turn us into slaves. We may feel as though our work is a form of slavery, or physical illness can restrict our lives. Often our society promises us freedom. Buy this product, and your problems will go away. Eat this; don't eat that. Do this; don't do that. And yet somehow we never *feel* free. What's promised never materializes. But when Jesus promises to set us free, He keeps His promise. As we follow Him, He will lead us into new paths, paths that lead to true freedom. All we have to do is follow Him—and say thank You over and over again.

———————

Jesus, thank You for setting me free.

Knit Together in Love

*That their hearts might be comforted, being knit
together in love, and unto all riches of the full assurance
of understanding, to the acknowledgement of the
mystery of God, and of the Father, and of Christ.*
COLOSSIANS 2:2 KJV

The comfort God gives us is another reason we have to feel gratitude. In this life, God will always be a mystery to us; we will never fully understand who He is. And that's a good thing, because God is too big for us to put Him into a box. As we acknowledge that truth, we gain new riches in understanding. We are knit together in love with others and with God. Then, even in the midst of trouble and confusion, our hearts will be comforted. We can thank God that even though there is so much we don't understand, we do understand that we are loved.

Thank You, God, for knitting my heart close to Yours.

What Comes Next

*We continue to shout our praise even when we're hemmed
in with troubles, because we know how troubles can
develop passionate patience in us, and how that patience
in turn forges the tempered steel of virtue, keeping us
alert for whatever God will do next. In alert expectancy
such as this, we're never left feeling shortchanged.*
ROMANS 5:3–5 MSG

When we "shout our praise," we're thanking God for all He has
done for us and *will* do for us. We usually think of gratitude as an
emotion we feel about something in the past or present, but the
Bible tells us to feel grateful for things that haven't yet happened.
During difficult times, we can be grateful for what we are learning and thankful for whatever God will do next. That attitude
of grateful expectancy brightens dark times and gives us hope.

Remind me, God, that You are always working.
Thank You for whatever You do next.

He Will Answer

I waited patiently for the LORD; and he
inclined unto me, and heard my cry.
He brought me up also out of an horrible pit.
PSALM 40:1–2 KJV

David found himself in a "horrible pit" with no way out, and he cried loudly to the Lord to rescue him. It took time for God to answer. David undoubtedly learned more patience in the process and probably had to endure doubts, wondering if God cared about the dilemma he was in.

Even Jeremiah didn't always get immediate answers to prayer. Once he and some Jewish refugees were in a dire situation, yet after Jeremiah prayed, the Lord took ten days to answer (Jeremiah 42:7). But the answer *did* come. . .in time.

Today we sometimes find ourselves in a "horrible pit" as well, and we pray desperately for God to bring us up out of it. He will. We often just need to be patient.

Help me to be patient with You, God.
I know that You will answer me. Amen.

Every Prayer

*LORD, thou hast heard the desire of
the humble: thou wilt prepare their
heart, thou wilt cause thine ear to hear.*
PSALM 10:17 KJV

Help! is a prayer every heart knows how to pray, even those who are unsure if there's a God who's listening. It's a cry that acknowledges that life is out of our control and a deep-seated hope that someone is ultimately in charge. Our desperate cries do not disappear into thin air. God hears every prayer, sees every tear, and doesn't hesitate to act. God's answers and timing are not always what we expect, but they are what we need.

What an amazing thought. . . You actually care
about and count my tears, Lord! I'm so grateful that
You are near and that You care. I love You, Lord!

Heavenly Riches

*You know the grace of our Lord Jesus Christ,
that though He was rich, yet for your sake He became
poor, so that you through His poverty might become rich.*
2 CORINTHIANS 8:9 NASB

Jesus gives us so many reasons to be grateful. Think about what it meant for Him to become a human. First, He set aside all the riches and power of heaven. He could have been born into an important wealthy family; He could have chosen to have earthly wealth and prestige. Instead, He became a poor person, a common laborer, someone people barely noticed for the first thirty years of His life. He did this so that He could identify with ordinary people. He did this so you and I could share His heavenly riches.

Thank You, Jesus, for becoming
poor so that I could be rich.

The Here and Now

I have learned to be content whatever the circumstances.
PHILIPPIANS 4:11 NIV

Sometimes we're so focused on the future that we forget to notice what we have right now in the present moment. We act as though happiness is always somewhere up ahead instead of finding it in the here and now. Having goals for the future can be healthy and productive, but at the same time we should learn to follow the apostle Paul's example and be content with the circumstances we've been given *now*. "Be grateful for what you already have while you pursue your goals," writes author Roy T. Bennett. "If you aren't grateful for what you already have, what makes you think you would be happy with more?"

Teach me, Lord, to be grateful for the here and now.

Divine Generosity

He gave us a good bath, and we came out of it new people, washed inside and out by the Holy Spirit. Our Savior Jesus poured out new life so generously. God's gift has restored our relationship with him and given us back our lives. And there's more life to come—an eternity of life!

TITUS 3:5–7 MSG

When your heart is full of complaints and worries, when your life feels small and restricted, spend time meditating on this verse. Write it on a note card and tape it somewhere you'll see it often. Read and reread it. Pray over it. Absorb this reality: Jesus has made us clean through the Holy Spirit; we are new people, free to live new lives. God is close to us in a new way, and all the riches of life still lie ahead. Divine generosity is everywhere we turn.

Lord, replace my worry and resentment with gratitude for all You have done for me.

Stillness

Be still, and know that I am God.
PSALM 46:10 NKJV

David wrote, "Meditate within your heart on your bed, and be still" (Psalm 4:4 NKJV). Many of us have lost the ability to meditate on God. We either tell ourselves that meditation is something only Buddhist monks do, or we cry out frantic prayers while distracted by the careening roller coaster of life. When we lie down in bed at night, instead of meditating calmly and trusting in God, we fret and toss and turn.

When we learn to trust that God can protect us and work out our problems, we can lie down peacefully and sleep (Psalm 4:8). That same trust gives us the strength to face our days with confidence.

Dear God, quiet my mind. Remove from it
all the worldly thoughts that come between
You and me. Create stillness within me,
and turn my thoughts toward You. Amen.

Beyond Intelligence

The fastest runner does not always win the race,
the strongest soldier does not always win the
battle, the wisest does not always have food. . . .
Time and chance happen to everyone.
ECCLESIASTES 9:11 NCV

How smart do you think you are? Do you assume you will be able to think your way through life's problems? Many of us do, but God reminds us that some things are beyond the scope of our intelligence. Some days life simply doesn't make sense. But even then, grace is there with us in the chaos. When we can find no rational answers to life's dilemmas, we have no choice but to rely absolutely on God.

God, I am conditioned to rely on strength, speed, and efficiency. While those things are useful, I know that wisdom is more important. Help me to seek answers directly from You. Amen.

The Words of Jesus

*"The words I have spoken to you—
they are full of the Spirit and life."*
JOHN 6:63 NIV

The words Jesus spoke to us in the Gospels can be another inspiration for our gratitude. How good it is that we have these records of the words He spoke when He was with us on earth! As we read and reread them, they sink into our hearts and minds. We gain access to the Spirit. We have a deeper understanding of life. We come alive in new and profound ways. We learn how to follow Jesus more closely. How grateful we should be that we have this glimpse into the mind and Spirit of Jesus! How good God is to have given us His Word where we can find the wisdom we need for life!

Jesus, thank You for the words You spoke while You walked this earth with physical feet. May I daily learn from You.

The Vine

*"I am the Vine, you are the branches.
When you're joined with me and I with you,
the relation intimate and organic, the harvest is
sure to be abundant. Separated, you can't produce a
thing. Anyone who separates from me is deadwood,
gathered up and thrown on the bonfire. But if you
make yourselves at home with me and my words
are at home in you, you can be sure that whatever
you ask will be listened to and acted upon."*

JOHN 15:5–7 MSG

Our connection to Jesus is something living and organic, even closer than the connections we share with family. Sometimes this relationship is referred to as the body of Christ, where each body part and organ is needed, all interdependent. But here Jesus uses the metaphor of the vine—living, green, and growing. Each of us draws our life from Jesus, makes our home in Jesus. How thankful we can be for this amazing intimacy with Christ!

Jesus, I am grateful for the living
relationship I have with You.

Forgiveness and Gratitude

*Then Peter came to Jesus and asked,
"Lord, how many times shall I forgive my
brother or sister who sins against me?
Up to seven times?" Jesus answered, "I tell
you, not seven times, but seventy-seven times."*

MATTHEW 18:21–22 NIV

At first glance, you might not think gratitude has much to do with forgiveness. But as Oprah Winfrey once said, "True forgiveness is when you can say, 'Thank you for that experience.'" Where there is a thankful heart, there is no room for unforgiveness. Gratitude lets go of resentment and anger. It replaces "That wasn't fair, God!" with "Thank You, Lord, for the chance to learn more about myself, about You, about others." Gratitude is a willingness to see the good even in what irks us or hurts us. It releases our need to be right. It surrenders to the will of God in every circumstance.

Teach me, Lord, to say thank You even when it's hard.

Living the Truth

Mark the perfect man, and behold the upright: for the end of that man is peace.
PSALM 37:37 KJV

Honesty is more than just telling the truth. It's living it. When you conform to the expectations of those around you instead of focusing on maturing into the individual God designed you to be, you rob the world of something priceless—the unique gift of you. You also rob yourself of the joy and freedom that come from fulfilling your God-given potential. When it comes to being the true you, honesty truly is the best policy.

Help me to bless my personality instead of curse it by trying so hard to conform to the personalities of others. Help me to live out exactly who You made me to be, Father.

Noisy Gratitude

Praise the LORD. Praise God in his sanctuary;
praise him in his mighty heavens. Praise him for
his acts of power; praise him for his surpassing
greatness. Praise him with the sounding of the
trumpet, praise him with the harp and lyre, praise
him with timbrel and dancing, praise him with
the strings and pipe, praise him with the clash of
cymbals, praise him with resounding cymbals.

PSALM 150:1–5 NIV

Sometimes gratitude is a quiet sort of emotion, a peaceful, calm feeling that fills our hearts when we are alone. Other times, we may want to express our thankfulness loudly and publicly. This verse from Psalms talks about noisy gratitude, the kind of thankfulness that bursts into song, that clangs cymbals, that blows trumpets, that dances and bangs and makes a ruckus. No matter how we praise Him, God loves to hear our voices!

May I praise You, Lord, both quietly
and loudly, every chance I get.

New!

Therefore, if anyone is in Christ, he is a new creation; old things have passed away, and look, new things have come. Everything is from God, who reconciled us to Himself through Christ and gave us the ministry of reconciliation.

2 Corinthians 5:17–18 HCSB

All of us have made mistakes. We may feel guilt for the times we have hurt others. We may also feel shame for things that have been done to us, things that made us feel small or soiled or broken. But in Christ, all those things are gone. We become brand-new people, ready for an all-new life in Christ. We are brought close to God and are given the work of helping others come close to God and to each other. The past no longer has the power to hurt us. Gratitude replaces shame and guilt.

Thank You, Jesus, for making me a new person, for giving me a new life.

Beloved Children

So you have not received a spirit that makes you fearful slaves. Instead, you received God's Spirit when he adopted you as his own children. Now we call him, "Abba, Father." For his Spirit joins with our spirit to affirm that we are God's children.

Romans 8:15–16 NLT

How thankful we can be that we are truly God's children! We may still refer to God as "Lord," as a term of respect, but God says that we are not servants or slaves; instead, we are His beloved children. We have the right to call God "Daddy"! The Holy Spirit within us joins with our own spirits, letting us know that we are loved, that we have an intimate relationship with the Creator of the universe. This is the reality we are called to experience as God's own children, our hearts overflowing with love, joy, and gratitude.

———————

Thank You, Father, that You have made me Your child.

God Already Knows

"As soon as you began to pray, a word went out,
which I have come to tell you, for you are highly esteemed."
DANIEL 9:23 NIV

In the middle of pouring out his heart to God one day, Daniel's prayer is interrupted by the appearance of the angel Gabriel. Bringing insight and understanding (v. 22), Gabriel's message contains the interesting concept that in the instant that Daniel began to pray, the answer was already on its way.

Before Daniel got past his salutation, God knew Daniel's heart and had already set in motion the response to Daniel's unfinished prayer.

As He did for Daniel, God knows our needs even before we give voice to them in prayer. We can rest in the knowledge that even before the words leave our lips, God has already heard them, and He has already answered them.

———

Thank You, God, for answering my prayers.
Before the words leave my lips, You already have the
answer. How great You are, God! I praise You. Amen.

God's Church

I will give thee thanks in the great congregation:
I will praise thee among much people.
PSALM 35:18 KJV

There's beauty and power in drawing close to God each morning to talk to Him about the day ahead. But you are just one of God's children. Sometimes it's great to get the family together for prayer and worship. Every Sunday, in churches around the world, that's exactly what's happening. God's family is getting together for a thanksgiving celebration. Like any family get-together, your presence adds to the joy. So join in! God's church wouldn't be the same without you.

Thank You for making me a part of the body of Christ.
What an amazing honor to be called Your daughter!
I join my family in praising You, heavenly Father.

Gifts That Keep Giving

*There are different kinds of spiritual gifts, but the
same Spirit is the source of them all. There are
different kinds of service, but we serve the same
Lord. God works in different ways, but it is the same
God who does the work in all of us. A spiritual gift
is given to each of us so we can help each other.*

1 CORINTHIANS 12:4–7 NLT

Gifts inspire gratitude. They are given freely, never earned; they
have no strings attached. And God loves to give. He hands out
gifts everywhere, and His gifts keep on giving. Through God,
we become a part of the never-ending celebration of giving and
gratitude. Just think about it! You have been given something that
allows you to show others who God is. It's your own unique gift,
given to you by God—and now you get to pass it on.

I am so grateful, God, for the gifts You have given
me. May I use Your gifts to show Your love to others.

Our Body

*No one ever hates his own flesh
but provides and cares for it.*
Ephesians 5:29 HCSB

Are you grateful for your body? Despite what this scripture verse says, too many of us have in fact been taught to hate our bodies. We hold them up against an impossible Barbie-doll standard, and when they fall short, we criticize them and feel shame. Our bodies, however, are amazing creations, capable of so many wonderful things. Consider thanking your body for its ability to move and for its amazing senses of sight, smell, hearing, touch, and taste. Be grateful for all the ways it serves you so faithfully. And express your gratitude by providing and caring for your body's needs.

Thank You, God, for this flesh You created.
May I honor it and care for it responsibly.

Wants and Needs

God will supply all your needs according to
His riches in glory in Christ Jesus.
PHILIPPIANS 4:19 NASB

Sometimes it's difficult to tell our wants from our needs. God never promises that we'll have everything that tickles our fancy, but the Bible does say that God will give us everything we truly need. We can count on Him to draw from His great eternal wealth on our behalf. The Greek word that's translated here as "glory" meant literally "brightness, splendor, the manifestation of God." Think about that! Through Jesus, we have direct access to the light that is God. Life may still be challenging, but we can be grateful that God is giving us exactly what we need when we need it.

I am so grateful, Jesus, that I can share
in Your splendor and light. Thank You
for giving me everything I need.

Full!

*"I have come that they may have
life, and have it to the full."*
JOHN 10:10 NIV

The life we have in Christ is not restricted or narrow. Grace doesn't flow to us in a meager trickle; it fills our life to the fullest. God's grace comes to us each moment, day after day, year after year, a generous flood that fills every crack and crevice of our lives and then overflows.

Jesus, I sometimes long so deeply for heaven
that I forget You have big plans for me
on this earth. Thank You that those plans
involve a rich and abundant life. Amen.

Hope

Happy is he that hath the God of Jacob for his help, whose hope is in the LORD his God.
PSALM 146:5 KJV

Some people place their hope in financial security. Others hope their popularity, abilities, or connections will get them where they want to go. Still others hope that if they want something badly enough, it'll just happen. But only those who place their hope in God can face tomorrow without any fear of the future. When you trust in God, you do more than hope for the best. You rest in knowing God's best is His plan for your life.

———————

My only hope is in You, Lord. Please make that the desire and the truth of my life. Forgive me for the times I hope in my own plans instead of Yours.

Don't Panic!

*"I, your GOD, have a firm grip on you
and I'm not letting go. I'm telling you,
'Don't panic. I'm right here to help you.'"*
ISAIAH 41:13 MSG

Life can be scary. Sometimes it seems as though we meet uncertainty and conflict everywhere we turn. It's easy to feel anxious, and some days we may find ourselves sinking into panic, asking ourselves if everything is going to turn out all right or if we and the rest of the world are heading for disaster. When you feel like that, make a point to read verses like this one. Let them soak into your mind. God has a firm grip on you! He will not drop you. You don't need to panic. Instead, you can let gratitude replace your fear and anxiety. . .and allow yourself to rest in God's capable hands.

You know, Lord, how frightening the world
is these days. Thank You that You are still
in control. Help me to trust You.

When We Are Weak

*Jotham strengthened himself because he did
not waver in obeying the LORD his God.*
2 CHRONICLES 27:6 HCSB

Do you ever feel too spiritually and emotionally weak to be grateful? We all have times like that, but the Bible tells us a secret: we will strengthen ourselves by obeying God, no matter how weak we may feel on the inside. In the Gospels, Jesus told us what it means to obey God. He said that all the commandments can be summed up in two simple things: to love God with all our hearts and minds, and to love others as ourselves (Matthew 22:37–39). As we make those two things the focus of our lives, our weakness will turn to strength, and our heart will once more spill over with gratitude for God's blessings.

When I am weak, Lord, remind me
to follow You more closely.

Inconceivably Magnificent

"No eye has seen, no ear has heard, and no mind has imagined what God has prepared for those who love him."
1 Corinthians 2:9 NLT

Despite all its problems, this world is a wonderful and beautiful place. But the Bible tells us that heaven will be incomparably more wonderful. We can't even imagine how lovely it will be. It's like trying to picture a color you've never seen or imagine a sense you don't have; we just can't come up with an image for something we've never seen or heard. Whatever we imagine will fall short of the reality we will one day discover. So when you feel grateful for this world's wondrous beauty, let your mind open to the unimaginable beauty of the next world, and thank God for all He has prepared for us there.

I can't imagine what heaven will be like, God, but I'm so glad that one day I'll find out!

Patience

Patient endurance is what you need now,
so that you will continue to do God's will.
Then you will receive all that he has promised.
HEBREWS 10:36 NLT

Life isn't all a bed of roses, and following Jesus won't automatically make life easier. Instead, the Bible tells us to let the hard times build our ability to endure. We learn to keep going, confident that God knows what He's doing, and to keep our eyes fixed on Him rather than the difficulties around us. Gratitude can help us develop patience. Even during the hard times, we can thank God for the way He is working behind the scenes, and we can anticipate what He is bringing into being for the future.

God, please teach me patience and
endurance. Help me to become the strong
follower You want me to be. And thank You,
Father, for all that You are doing all the time.

Call on Him in Faith

*"Call to me and I will answer you and tell you
great and unsearchable things you do not know."*
JEREMIAH 33:3 NIV

Jeremiah 33:3 says if we pray to God, He will answer us with wisdom. In the King James Version of the Bible, the word *pray* is used more than five hundred times. God wants us to pray. When we call on Him in prayer, we know that He hears us (1 John 5:15).

Proverbs 2:6 (NASB) says, "For the LORD gives wisdom; from His mouth come knowledge and understanding." God knows us fully, and He is able to direct us in wisdom and guide us through the works of His Holy Spirit.

Just as God gave Jeremiah wisdom when he prayed, He will do the same for you if you call on Him in faith (James 1:5–6).

God, I need Your help. I've sought counsel for my problem, and still I'm not sure what to do. But You know! Please, God, guide me with Your wisdom. Amen.

Increase in Value

*Be not thou afraid when one is made rich,
when the glory of his house is increased.*
PSALM 49:16 KJV

It's been said that "money talks." Sometimes it yells. Loudly. The things it buys helps draw attention to those who have it and to those who would do anything to get it. But money says absolutely nothing about who a person really is or how rich he or she truly is. You have riches that exceed what's in your bank account. Every relationship you invest in, be it with God, family, or friends, is a treasure that increases in value over time.

Father, thank You for teaching me that my
value has nothing to do with the money I make.
I am simply valuable because I'm Your child.

Waiting on the Lord

They that wait upon the LORD shall renew their strength;
they shall mount up with wings as eagles; they shall run,
and not be weary; and they shall walk, and not faint.
ISAIAH 40:31 KJV

When life seems exhausting, how do we renew our strength? The Bible tells us there's a secret to this: we wait upon the Lord. The Hebrew word that is translated "wait" meant literally "to eagerly expect, to look eagerly, to wait patiently." That's what it takes to keep us going when life is overwhelming: a patient eagerness for God. Even when our lives seem dry and empty, we can continue to look eagerly for God's presence. Doing so will give us new strength. We can rejoice in our ability to keep walking, running, and even flying. We can thank God for giving us the strength we need to keep going.

When I'm weary, Lord, remind me to wait
for You. Give me an eager expectation
as I place my confidence in You.

The Very Best

*"But if you remain in me and my words
remain in you, you may ask for anything
you want, and it will be granted!"*
JOHN 15:7 NLT

Is that true? As silly as this may sound, some assume that they can treat God as a concierge, standing by to fulfill their every request.

As we present our requests to God, we must realize that He knows what is best for us and that we should never demand "our way." We must not forget the first part of John 15:7 that says, "If you remain in me and my words remain in you." This should clearly tell us that our first desires need to be that God's will be done.

Since God only wants to give us the very best, and He knows how to make that happen, why would we pray for anything else?

Father, I say, "Thy will be done!" You
know best. I want what *You* want for me,
even if it's not what I ask for. Amen.

Reconnect

The Lord is nigh unto them that are of a broken heart; and saveth such as be of a contrite spirit.
PSALM 34:18 KJV

It's easy to lose heart when your focus is on difficulties that persist day after day. That's why reconnecting with God every morning is so important. Time together reminds you that an all-knowing and all-powerful God is in your corner, ready and able to help. It helps you sift the trivial from the eternal. And it restores hope to its rightful place in your life, where it can shine a light on God's goodness and faithfulness to you.

When I'm broken, I praise You that You come close to me. I trust that You are near and that You will comfort me in every pain and difficulty.

First Things First

*"Do not worry then, saying, 'What are we to eat?'
or 'What are we to drink?' or 'What are we to wear
for clothing?'. . . But seek first His kingdom and His
righteousness, and all these things will be provided to you."*
MATTHEW 6:31, 33 NASB

It's easy to worry about material things. Maybe we have enough to eat and drink, but we still worry about the bills piling up. We worry that we won't have enough to provide for our families. Jesus understood those concerns, and He told us, "Don't worry about those things! Instead, focus on My kingdom. When you do, I'll take care of the rest." How do we cultivate this attitude when worries are everywhere we turn? Once again, the answer is gratitude. Instead of worrying, thank God that He is caring for our material needs.

———————————

I am so grateful, Jesus, that You understand my
financial concerns. Help me to give them to You so
I can be free to help You build Your kingdom.

Nature

*May the heavens be joyful, and may the earth
rejoice; may the sea roar, and all it contains;
may the field be jubilant, and all that is in it.
Then all the trees of the forest will sing for joy.*
PSALM 96:11–12 NASB

Our modern age often thinks of nature as inanimate, without emotion or knowledge, but the Bible describes it as actively praising God with its very being. When gratitude seems difficult to drum up, going out into nature may help. There, beneath a blue sky or towering clouds, in fields of waving grass and wildflowers, amid the green silence of a forest, or on a beach roaring with the sound of the surf, we can join in the song of praise that rises up from all creation.

Lord, I praise You for the beautiful world You made.
May I take time to be in it and learn from it.

Call on Me

"Call on me in the day of trouble;
I will deliver you, and you will honor me."
PSALM 50:15 NIV

When God says He wants us to call Him, He means it. He must lean closer, bending His ear, waiting, longing for the sound of His name coming from our lips. He stands ready to deliver us from our troubles or at least to carry us through them safely.

While He doesn't always choose to fix things with a snap of His fingers, we can be assured that He will see us through to the other side of our troubles by a smoother path than we'd travel without Him. He's waiting to help us. All we have to do is call.

Dear Father, I'm so glad I can call on You
anytime with any kind of trouble. Amen.

The Center of Our Lives

*The apostles often met together and prayed
with a single purpose in mind.*
ACTS 1:14 CEV

What do you do when you get together with the people you're close to? You probably talk and laugh, share a meal, maybe go shopping or work on a project. But do you ever pray together? If prayer is the center of our lives, we will want to share this gift of grace with those with whom we're closest.

———————

Heavenly Father, when I meet together regularly
with my sisters and brothers, nudge us to pray
with a single purpose, keeping You in the
center and uniting us with Your love. Amen.

Quiet Time

Be still before the Lord, and wait patiently for him.
PSALM 37:7 NRSV

Our lives are busy. Responsibilities crowd our days, and at night as we go to bed, our minds often continue to be preoccupied with the day's work, ticking off a mental to-do list even as we fall asleep. We need to set aside time to quiet our hearts. In those moments, we can let go of all our to-dos and wait for God's grace to act in our lives.

God, thank You for this verse that reminds me of the gift of stillness. In my all-too-few quiet moments, help me to learn to wait patiently for You. Amen.

Work

God will lavish you with good things. . .
and bless the work you take in hand.
DEUTERONOMY 28:11–12 MSG

Our work is another reason to be grateful to God. Whether it's the job that allows us to earn our living, a creative activity like sewing or painting or writing a poem, or the daily work of caring for a home and a family, God is there with us in every task we take on. With each one, we have the opportunity to serve and praise God with our actions, no matter how ordinary they may seem. Through our work, God blesses both us and others. Perhaps we should make a habit, then, of thanking God as we begin each workday or at the outset of each new project. Just as we ask a blessing on our food, we could get in the habit of "saying grace" for our work as well.

Thank You for my work, Lord God.
May I do it to Your glory.

Beyond Our Imagination

[God] is able to do above and beyond all that we ask
or think according to the power that works in us.
EPHESIANS 3:20 HCSB

God may not answer our prayers just the way we had hoped, but when we look back at our lives, we can see that He was doing something better all along. He's not a magic genie who will grant our wishes; His plans for us are not limited by our imaginations. He will do so much more than we'd hoped or dreamed. We can be grateful that our thoughts put no boundaries on His actions. His power is unfathomable, and His creativity is boundless! Who knows what He will do next?

Thank You, beloved God, that You are doing
amazing things in my life. I am eagerly
waiting to see what You will do today.

Relax. . .

But I am calm and quiet, like a baby with its mother.
I am at peace, like a baby with its mother.
PSALM 131:2 NCV

You know how a baby lies completely limp in her mother's arms, totally trusting and at peace? That is the attitude you need to practice. Let yourself relax in God's arms, wrapped in His grace. Life will go on around you, with all its noise and turmoil. Meanwhile, you are completely safe, totally secure, without a worry in the world. Lie back and enjoy the quiet!

———————————

Heavenly Father, thank You for the peace You provide. Thank You that I can rest so gently and comfortably in Your loving arms. Amen.

True Humility

*Though the LORD be high, yet hath he respect unto
the lowly: but the proud he knoweth afar off.*
PSALM 138:6 KJV

Beloved child, rebellious daughter; faithful friend, self-centered
competitor; fully forgiven, fickle and flawed; priceless miracle,
nothing but dust: you are the sum of all these things and more.
Acknowledging that you're a crazy quilt of weakness and strength
is a step toward humility. After all, true humility isn't regarding
yourself as less significant than others. It's seeing yourself the
way God does, as no more or less than you truly are.

Father, help me see myself the way You
see me. Knowing that I have done nothing
to deserve the amazing gift of Christ's
righteousness, yet You love me still. Amazing!

Amen

*"Amen, blessing, glory, wisdom, thanksgiving,
honor, power, and might belong to our
God forever and ever. Amen."*
REVELATION 7:12 NASB

When we say "amen," we are saying, "Let it be so." We are affirming that God knows what He is doing and that His words are true and dependable. As a way of practicing gratitude, we might make a habit of saying "amen" at odd moments throughout the day—when the traffic light turns red as we are rushing to work, when we sit down to pay our bills, or when our spouse exasperates us. "Amen" may be the last thing we feel like saying in those circumstances, but in doing so, we let God know we are open to whatever He wants to do in our lives. We are letting go of our impatience, anxiety, and frustration, and we are saying, "Thank You for making this circumstance exactly the way it is."

Teach me, Lord, to say "amen" to
each thing You bring into my life.

Peace

*You will keep in perfect peace all who trust in
you, all whose thoughts are fixed on you!*
ISAIAH 26:3 NLT

So many things can steal our peace, but it's not the actual circumstances that rob us of the peace of mind we crave. Instead, it's our reactions to those circumstances. Worry, frustration, anger, resentment, jealousy, boredom—all these things can push peace out of our hearts. The solution is to respond instead to each circumstance with a "thank You, Lord," which will turn our thoughts to God. Responding this way also increases our trust, helping us to grow in faith even in the midst of difficult circumstances. When our thoughts are fixed on God, He will send His peace into our hearts.

May I know Your perfect peace, Lord,
no matter what is happening in my life.

Hannah's Prayer

"The eyes of the LORD search the whole earth in order to strengthen those whose hearts are fully committed to him."
2 CHRONICLES 16:9 NLT

Hannah was barren. She prayed before God and promised God that if He gave her a child, she would commit him to the Lord forever. God answered her prayer, granting Hannah a male child whom she named Samuel. After only a short time, she took him to Eli, the priest. Samuel was not an ordinary child. He heard the voice of God at a very young age. He grew up to become a judge and prophet who could not be matched in all of Israel's history.

God is looking for ordinary men and women whose prayers reflect hearts completely committed to Him. He found such commitment in Hannah, and He answered her prayer.

———————

Father, may my prayers reflect a deep commitment to You, and may all that I ask for be for Your kingdom and not for my own glory. Amen.

All Equal—By Grace

*Live in peace with each other. Do not be
proud, but make friends with those who seem
unimportant. Do not think how smart you are.*
ROMANS 12:16 NCV

Sometimes other people just seem so stupid! We pride ourselves
that we would never act like that, dress like that, talk like that. But
God wants us to let go of our pride. He wants us to remember
that in His eyes we are all equal, all loved, all saved only by grace.

Lord, Your Word is clear—pride keeps
me from living at peace with others.
Cleanse me from pride, and help me to
focus on loving instead of judging. Amen.

Rooted in Love

I pray that you, being rooted and established in love, may have power, together with all the Lord's holy people, to grasp how wide and long and high and deep is the love of Christ, and to know this love that surpasses knowledge—that you may be filled to the measure of all the fullness of God.
EPHESIANS 3:17–19 NIV

It's difficult enough to believe in someone we've never seen, let alone believe that someone loves us. Some days it may be easier to believe, while other days we may need to rely on the faith of other people to help us believe. Either way, as we make gratitude to God our way of life, our roots continually grow deeper into love. We will never be able to fully understand it or grasp it, but we can nevertheless experience it. We can become filled up with the fullness of God. Isn't that amazing?

Fill me with You, God. I want my roots to sink deep into Your love.

Light in the Dark

We also have the prophetic message as something completely reliable, and you will do well to pay attention to it. . . . Above all, you must understand that no prophecy of Scripture came about by the prophet's own interpretation of things. For prophecy never had its origin in the human will, but prophets, though human, spoke from God as they were carried along by the Holy Spirit.

2 PETER 1:19–21 NIV

Do you ever wonder if the people who wrote the Bible really knew what they were talking about? Doubt is a normal thing, but here Peter is telling us that we can believe the Bible's account of Jesus and His love. When we cannot *feel* God, we can cling to verses like these. While we wait to see Jesus face-to-face, we can thank Him for His words of life and love as recorded in the Bible.

Thank You, Jesus, for Your Word. Teach me to focus on it so that it lights up even my dark times.

Keep Talking

The LORD is near to all who call on him,
to all who call on him in truth.
PSALM 145:18 NIV

When we call on God, no matter our circumstances, we become close to Him. He sees our hearts, He has compassion on us, and He longs to pull us into His arms and hold us there. When we call on Him, when we spend time talking to Him and telling Him what's on our minds, we strengthen our relationship with Him. We get *close* to Him.

When we feel far from God, sometimes the last thing we want to do is talk to Him. But it is through honest, heartfelt conversation, however one-sided it may seem to us, that we draw into God's presence. When we feel far from God, we need to keep talking. He's there.

Dear Father, thank You for Your promise
to listen to me. I love You, I need You,
and I want to be close to You. Amen.

Always Present

> LORD, *you have been watching.*
> *Do not keep quiet. Lord, do not leave me alone.*
> PSALM 35:22 NCV

Have you ever seen a child suddenly look up from playing, realize she's all alone, and then run to get her mother's attention? Meanwhile, her mother was watching her all along. Sometimes solitude is a good thing, and other times, it's just plain lonely. When loneliness turns into isolation, remember that God's loving eyes are always on you. He will never leave you all alone, and His grace is always present.

Lord, how wonderful to know that You are always with me, watching over me with tender, loving eyes. Help me to listen to Your voice, remembering I am never alone. Amen.

Steering Wheel

And in thy majesty ride prosperously because of truth and meekness and righteousness; and thy right hand shall teach thee terrible things.

PSALM 45:4 KJV

Remembering that only God is God keeps us humble. Sounds simple enough. But all too often we try to grab the wheel from God's hands and steer our lives in the direction of what looks like it will make us happy instead of simply doing what God asks us to do. Invite God to expose any areas of your life where pride has you heading in the wrong direction. Ask Him to reveal to you how big He really is.

———————————

Lord, help me to be still and know that You alone are God. Show me how big and all-powerful You are. . . and at the same time so intimate and loving.

Careful Plans

Without good advice everything goes wrong—
it takes careful planning for things to go right.
PROVERBS 15:22 CEV

The Bible reminds us that when we start a new venture, we should not trust success to come automatically. We need to seek the advice of those we trust. We need to make careful plans. Most of all, we need to seek God's counsel, praying for the grace and wisdom to do things right.

Father, there are so many opportunities for me to grab hold of. It's tempting to dive in head first. I desperately need Your counsel. Fill me with Your grace and wisdom. Amen.

A Thanksgiving Chorus

Give thanks to the LORD, for He is good,
for His mercy is everlasting.
PSALM 107:1 NASB

The theme of Psalm 107 is expressed in this first verse. The verses that follow give four reasons to give God thanks. Each instance begins with a cry of distress over the situation in which the people found themselves, followed by a summary of how God heard and answered prayer. At the end of each, the "thanksgiving chorus" that begins the psalm is repeated once again. We too can experience this pattern in our own lives, crying out for God's help and then singing our thanksgiving chorus when we see His deliverance.

You are so good, Lord.
Your love and kindness never end.

Our Children

"I will pour out my Spirit on your descendants,
and my blessing on your children."
ISAIAH 44:3 NLT

It's easy to feel anxious about the children in our lives. After all, the world is full of dangers over which we have no control. The older our children grow, the less control we have. We worry about the decisions they may make; we wonder if they are safe and happy and healthy. But God has promised to bless our children. We can put them in His hands, thanking Him for His faithfulness and care. Just as He has blessed us and led us, so He also will lead our children. We can trust Him to pour out His Spirit on them.

Thank You for the children in my
life, Lord, and thank You that You
love them even more than I do.

Staying on Track

*I have fought a good fight, I have finished
my course, I have kept the faith.*
2 Timothy 4:7 KJV

Despite the pain and afflictions Paul suffered in his life, he kept his eyes on Jesus, using praise to commune with God.

Likewise, we can keep in constant communion with the Father. We are so blessed to have been given the Holy Spirit within to keep us in tune with His will. Through His guidance, that still, small voice, we can rest assured our priorities will stay focused on Jesus. As the author A. W. Tozer wrote, "Lord, guide me carefully on this uncharted sea. . .as I daily seek You in Your word. Then use me mightily as Your servant this year as I boldly proclaim Your word in leading others."

Lord, no better words have been spoken than
to say I surrender to Your will. Amen.

Praying Together

*For where two or three are gathered together in
my name, there am I in the midst of them.*
MATTHEW 18:20 KJV

Of all the passages in the Bible that emphasize the importance of gathering for worship and prayer, this one stands out. It is short and sweet and to the point. Why should we gather together to pray with other Christians? Because when we do, *God shows up!* The Lord is in our midst.

As you gather with other Christians in your church or even in your family, God is honored. He loves to listen to the hearts and voices of His children unified in prayer. He will be faithful to answer according to His perfect will.

Father, thank You for the promise that
where we gather in Your name, there You will
be also. Help me never to give up the practice
of praying with fellow believers. Amen.

Wordless

Unless the LORD had been my help,
my soul had almost dwelt in silence.
PSALM 94:17 KJV

Sometimes life's situations stun us into silence. We're too overwhelmed to say thank You to God. We can't even manage to cry out for help. And yet even then, the Bible says that God will help us. He won't leave us in silence. His Spirit's quiet urging will pull our hearts to Him. The Spirit will even pray on our behalf with "groanings that cannot be expressed in words" (Romans 8:26 NLT). Eventually, He will give us the strength we need to put words to our situation. Once again we will be able to voice our gratitude to God.

Thank You, Lord of love, that You do
not leave my soul in silence.

Perfectly Forgiving

*For thou, Lord, art good, and ready to forgive;
and plenteous in mercy unto all them that call upon thee.*
PSALM 86:5 KJV

The fact that God is perfect can be intimidating, especially when you consider that God knows everything you've ever done. But our perfect God is also perfectly forgiving. There is nothing you can do or have done that will make Him turn away from you. When you ask for forgiveness, you have it. No groveling. No begging. All you need to do is come to Him in humility and truth. Jesus has taken care of the rest.

I'm so amazed at Your great love for me, Lord God! You can never love me more or less than You do right now. Thank You for Your grace and love in my life.

Prince of Peace

The peace of God, which transcends all understanding,
will guard your hearts and your minds in Christ Jesus.
PHILIPPIANS 4:7 NIV

When we focus on things we can't do anything about, we end up feeling frustrated and worried. We lose our sense of peace. When we fret about things beyond our control, stress and tension can make us not only upset and anxious but even physically ill. Worry seems to come naturally enough, but let it be a cue that reminds us to turn our thoughts immediately to gratitude. In other words, each time we sense ourselves beginning to struggle with anxiety or frustration, we can quickly shift our focus to gratitude instead. As we make a habit of shifting our focus, God's peace, which goes beyond human understanding, will guard our thoughts.

Thank You, Prince of peace, for Your constant
care. Remind me to turn to thanksgiving
whenever anxiety overtakes me.

Light

Ye are the light of the world.
A city that is set on an hill cannot be hid.
MATTHEW 5:14 KJV

A lot of people have negative ideas about what Christians are like. Unfortunately, they often get those ideas from observing how Christians behave. Christians who are hypocritical in their actions and beliefs confuse people. Christians who are gloomy, angry, or judgmental can cause others to think that's what it means to follow Christ. But the Bible asks us to be light for the world. In today's tense and polarized world, being the light that we're called to be is even more important. May others see us shining with gratitude, joy, and love!

Make me shine for You, Lord.

At Home in Your Heart

*They also that dwell in the uttermost parts are
afraid at thy tokens: thou makest the outgoings
of the morning and evening to rejoice.*

PSALM 65:8 KJV

Happiness is usually the result of circumstance. Joy, however, bubbles up unbidden, often persisting in spite of circumstance. It's an excitement that simmers below the surface, an assurance that God is working behind the scenes, a contentment that deepens as you discover your place in the world. The more at home you feel with God, the more joy will make a home in your heart—a welcome reminder that God is near.

Fill me with joy as I continue to seek
Your presence, heavenly Father. I want to
understand and exhibit joy in my relationships,
reminding everyone that You are near.

Open Up!

*"It was I, the LORD your God, who
rescued you. . . . Open your mouth wide,
and I will fill it with good things."*
PSALM 81:10 NLT

Sometimes we put limits on God. We don't believe He can change
our situations. We doubt He can heal our wounds or break our
bad habits. We think our circumstances are hopeless. But God
asks us to remember all the ways He has rescued us in the past.
And then He says, "Open your mouth wide! Stop nibbling at My
grace when I have an abundance I'm waiting to give you. Don't
put limits on Me. I want to fill your life with good things. Just
wait and see all the ways I'm going to bless you. So open up!"

Thank You, Lord, that nothing is hopeless to You.
Help me to be open to Your amazing grace.

Old Age

*I was young and now I am old, yet I have never seen
the righteous forsaken or their children begging bread.*
PSALM 37:25 NIV

Do you ever worry about your old age? Are you afraid of the ways
your body may fail you? Do you fret about how your children
will manage when you are too old to be there for them, when
you may have to rely on them instead of the other way around?
In this verse, the psalmist asks us to pay attention to his witness.
He knows from experience God does not abandon anyone in
their old age, nor will He leave their children without the help
they need. God will never ever forsake us or our children. We
can trust the future to Him and thank Him for the lifetime of
blessings He has planned for us.

Thank You, loving God, that You will be with
me when I am old. Thank You that You will
never forsake me or the people I love.

Powerful Praying

*Therefore confess your sins to each other and pray
for each other so that you may be healed. The prayer
of a righteous person is powerful and effective.*

JAMES 5:16 NIV

When we have God's approval, when we live with integrity and faith, He listens to us. But when we consistently make poor choices and disregard God's guidance, He may not take our prayers as seriously.

Oh, He will never take His love from us, no matter what. And He will always listen when we ask for help out of our sin. But if we want our prayers to hold extra power, we need to live righteously. When we have God's approval on our lives, we can also know we have God's ear about all sorts of things. When we walk in God's will, we have access to God's power.

Dear Father, I want my prayers to be
powerful and effective. Help me to live
in a way that pleases You. Amen.

Meant to Move

We are only foreigners living here on earth for a while, just as our ancestors were. And we will soon be gone, like a shadow that suddenly disappears.
1 CHRONICLES 29:15 CEV

We are not meant to feel too at home in this world. Maybe that is why time is designed to keep us from lingering too long in one place. We are meant to be moving on, making our way to our forever home in heaven. Grace has brought us safe thus far and grace will lead us home.

Father, the old song says, "This world is not my home, I'm just passing through. . . ." How I long for the treasure of my heavenly home. I cannot wait to be there with You. Amen.

Spirit Work

*It is God who is working in you, enabling you both
to desire and to work out His good purpose.*
PHILIPPIANS 2:13 HCSB

Sometimes we think that God expects us to pull ourselves up by our own bootstraps. We act as though it's all up to us—and when we fail, as we always do sooner or later, then we're filled with guilt. God wants us to stop trying so hard and relax into Him. God is the one who does the work, not us. God's Spirit is the one who even makes us *want* to do His will, and He's the one who will continue to work in our lives and in our hearts, shaping us into the people we were created to be. As we rely more and more on Him, as we turn to Him daily in gratitude, He will do amazing things in our lives.

Lord, shape me into the person You want me to be.
Teach me to surrender to Your Spirit at work in my life.

Crossroads

I've brought you today to the
crossroads of Blessing and Curse.
DEUTERONOMY 11:26 MSG

Sooner or later, we all stand at this crossroads. Will we go the way of God's blessing or will we stubbornly choose our own way and suffer the consequences? God never wants to curse us. He never wishes that painful or destructive things enter our lives. Always, always, He yearns to bless us. But sometimes our own actions lead to unavoidably negative results. Even then, God does not abandon us. The Bible tells the story of God's people getting off track over and over, and over and over He draws them back to Himself and gets them back on course. He'll do the same for us.

Oh Lord, thank You that when I make wrong choices, even then You do not abandon me.

Hope

*I pray that God, the source of hope, will fill you
completely with joy and peace because you trust
in him. Then you will overflow with confident
hope through the power of the Holy Spirit.*

ROMANS 15:13 NLT

This word, *hope*, means "the expectation of something good."
Notice in this verse that hope is not something we're supposed
to work up in ourselves; instead, it *comes from God*. He gives
us the confidence to believe we can trust Him. His Spirit in
us gives us power to overflow with hope! Living hope-filled
lives means we're constantly expecting God to bless us—and
He will. He will give us more and more reasons to be grateful,
for hope and gratitude go hand in hand. We expect something
good—and we're grateful for it, even ahead of time.

———————

I am so grateful, Spirit of God,
for the power You give me to hope.

An Empty Chalkboard

*As far as the east is from the west, so far hath
he removed our transgressions from us.*
PSALM 103:12 KJV

Picture a chalkboard. Written on it is everything you've ever
done that goes against what God has asked of you. What would
you see written there? How big would the chalkboard be? Now
imagine God wiping it clean with one swipe of His hand. Nothing
remains, not the faintest image of one single word. That's how
completely God has forgiven you. When guilt or shame over
past mistakes threatens to creep back into your life, remember
the empty chalkboard—and rejoice.

I cannot praise You enough for cleaning my
slate, Lord Jesus. The truth of who You are
and what You've done are astonishing to
me. I put my whole heart in Your hands.

Gratitude Feasts

Feast there in the Presence of GOD, your God.
Celebrate everything that you and your families have
accomplished under the blessing of GOD, your God.
DEUTERONOMY 12:7 MSG

Sometimes we need to take time for special moments of gratitude, celebrations of all God has done for us and our families and all we have accomplished. Maybe we do this on Thanksgiving or at Christmas, but it might also be good to have more informal celebrations, our own intimate gatherings of gratitude. Maybe we'll invite friends and extended family, or maybe it will be just our immediate families, sharing a special meal. Maybe we want to go for a walk by ourselves or spend time alone, remembering all the blessings God has given us. However we choose to celebrate, these "gratitude feasts" can be times of remembrance that strengthen our hearts for the days ahead.

You have blessed us in so many ways, Creator God,
and You have helped us accomplish so much!

Playful Spirits

*"But for you who revere my name, the sun of
righteousness will rise with healing in its rays.
And you will go out and frolic like well-fed calves."*
Malachi 4:2 niv

Some days, it may seem as though we carry the weight of the
world upon our shoulders. We plod along, our steps heavy and
our hearts even heavier. But God doesn't want us to linger in
these dreary times. Instead, He wants to shine His light on us.
He yearns to heal us and lift our heavy loads; He wants to nourish
our spirits and bodies, making them both healthy. And not only
does He long to make us happy, but He also wants to give us
spirits so joyful that we feel like playing like children again. And
He will do all these things as we turn to Him, revering His name.

God, when I'm downhearted, remind me that You
are already planning ways to bless me yet again,
so that one day soon, I'll feel like playing.

A Blossoming Spirit

A cheerful heart is good medicine,
but a broken spirit saps a person's strength.
PROVERBS 17:22 NLT

Some of us seem to be born with naturally optimistic and cheery natures, while others struggle with pessimism and negativity. If you're one of the "Eeyore" sorts of people, always sighing and seeing the dark side of life, you can counteract this tendency. You can form new thought habits, focusing on all there is to be grateful for in life. You can make a list of things you're thankful for and refer to it often. Or you can keep a gratitude journal, daily jotting down everything good, even the littlest things, that happened that day. Make a habit of telling God thank You often, and you may find that your cheerful spirit will begin to blossom.

———————

Give me a cheerful spirit, Lord.
Make me strong in Your joy.

Justice

The mouth of the righteous speaketh wisdom,
and his tongue talketh of judgment.
PSALM 37:30 KJV

It takes courage to stand up for what's right, especially if you're the only voice speaking up in the crowd. But words have power. They can help bring injustice to light. They can encourage others to take a stand. They can incite change. But the right motive is just as important as the right words. Ephesians 4:15 tells us to speak "the truth in love." Truth tempered with love is the perfect agent of change.

Lord, help me to stand up for injustice.
Give me courage and boldness to speak and
the wisdom to know when the time is right.

The Natural World

*"The wild animals honor me, the jackals
and the owls, because I provide water in the
wilderness and streams in the wasteland."*
ISAIAH 43:20 NIV

Take a moment to think about the wild animals that live around you. We are often unaware of these busy lives, worms munching through the soil, birds eating worms, and squirrels burying nuts in the earth—and foxes and hawks consuming birds and squirrels. The Bible says that all these creatures honor God with their lives—and in return, He provides for them. Our world is made so intricately, with each aspect of nature interdependent with all the rest, and we too are part of that interwoven web. May we appreciate nature as the gift from God that it truly is, and may we honor God's world as it honors Him!

Thank You, Creator, for the natural world
around me. Teach me to see it with fresh eyes,
and show me ways to care for it responsibly.

Desert Times

> *"I will open up rivers for them on the high plateaus. I will give them fountains of water in the valleys. I will fill the desert with pools of water. Rivers fed by springs will flow across the parched ground."*
>
> ISAIAH 41:18 NLT

We all have times in our lives that seem dry and barren. We may have trouble seeing any reasons to feel grateful. Maybe our life's circumstances are hard and challenging; maybe nothing is wrong, yet our emotions seem to have dried up inside us, leaving everything looking a little flat and bleak. Whatever the case, we can cling to promises like the one found in this verse. God will not leave us forever in these desert times. Soon He will refresh us with pools of grace and rivers of His mercy. We just have to be patient.

Teach me, Father, to wait for Your grace and mercy watering my life. I thank You for all You are doing, even in the dry, barren times of my life.

Giving

Give freely and spontaneously. Don't have a stingy heart. The way you handle matters like this triggers God, *your God's, blessing in everything you do, all your work and ventures. There are always going to be poor and needy people among you. So I command you: Always be generous, open purse and hands, give to your neighbors in trouble, your poor and hurting neighbors.*

DEUTERONOMY 15:10–11 MSG

Gratitude works well with other qualities. Another quality that could be seen as the flip side of gratitude is generosity. We have been given so much—now God asks us to give as freely as we have received. Our generous God wants us to pass along His blessings to others; He wants us to reflect His self-giving love to everyone we meet. This is the best way we can express gratitude for all we have been given.

Generous God, give me opportunities today to give to others. You have given me so much. May I be equally as generous in my interactions with everyone I encounter.

Fresh and Green

The righteous will flourish like a palm tree, they will grow like a cedar of Lebanon; planted in the house of the LORD, they will flourish in the courts of our God. They will still bear fruit in old age, they will stay fresh and green.

PSALM 92:12–14 NIV

God never stops blessing us. He has always been with us, always close by even when we did not feel His presence. Looking back, we are filled with gratitude; we can look forward with the same thankfulness for God will continue to bless us throughout our lives. This verse promises that even in old age, we will bear "fruit"; we will remain "fresh and green," despite the years. We will not just survive; we will flourish!

Thank You, God of love, that You have been with me throughout my life, and thank You that I can anticipate the years ahead, even into old age, with grateful eagerness for the new ways You will bless me.

Growing in Grace

*This is my prayer for you: that your love
will grow more and more; that you will have
knowledge and understanding with your love.*
PHILIPPIANS 1:9 NCV

God wants us to be spiritually mature. He wants us to love more deeply, and at the same time, He wants us to reach deeper into wisdom and understanding. This is not something we can accomplish in our own strength with our own abilities. Only God can make us grow in grace.

———————

God, I long for my love to grow more and more.
Fill me with knowledge and understanding; help me
to lean into Your grace that brings growth. Amen.

Ups and Downs

Is anyone among you suffering? Then he must pray. Is anyone cheerful? He is to sing praises.
JAMES 5:13 NASB

Are you having a "blue" day when nothing looks right and everything seems wrong? Take it to God in prayer. Tell Him your feelings. Or are you having one of those days when the whole world seems to smile and you find yourself humming as you go about your work? Take that to God as well; lift your heart up to Him in praise and gratitude. Each emotion you feel can be a tether tugging your heart closer to the Lord. As you make a habit of telling God what you're feeling, you may find that your emotions no longer sway your heart to and fro. Instead, you'll have an inner steadiness that relies on God no matter what your emotions may be.

———

Thank You for the gift of my emotions, God.
May I remember to give each one of them to You.

When We're Depressed

God, who comforts the depressed,
comforted us by the coming of Titus.
2 CORINTHIANS 7:6 NASB

Many times, God uses other people to bless us and lift us when we're feeling down. Even the apostle Paul experienced this. He was encouraged and strengthened when his good friend Titus joined him. God will do the same for us when we are downhearted. Good friends who care and listen to our troubles can lift our hearts with their understanding. Sometimes even a smile from a stranger at just the right moment can make all the difference. All we have to do is open our hearts to the individuals God brings into our lives, and then remember to thank God for blessing us through other people.

Lord, when I am feeling sad and
dreary, please send along someone who
understands, someone who can help.

Building God's Kingdom

*"I have filled him with the Spirit of God,
with wisdom, with understanding, with
knowledge and with all kinds of skills."*
EXODUS 31:3 NIV

Your abilities, your intelligence, your knowledge, and your talents
are all gifts of grace from God's generous Spirit. But without
wisdom, the ability to see into the spiritual world, none of these
gifts is worth very much. Wisdom is what fits together all of
the other pieces, allowing us to use our talents to build God's
spiritual kingdom.

Lord, I am so grateful for the filling of Your Spirit and
for the gift of wisdom. Thank You for allowing me to
be involved with the building of Your kingdom. Amen.

Others' Hearts

O taste and see that the LORD is good:
blessed is the man that trusteth in him.
PSALM 34:8 KJV

Kindness turns criticism into encouragement, bad news into words of comfort, and discipline into teachable moments. That's because kindness is concerned with more than results. It's also concerned with people's hearts. God's plan for you is bigger than being a "good person." God also wants you to be healed and whole. You can trust God to be a loving Father and not a callous taskmaster because the breadth of His kindness stems from the depth of His love.

Father, I praise You that You came to heal my heart and set me free! Your kindness is unwavering. Pour Your kindness into me so I can in turn pour kindness into others.

Prayer

A prayer of a righteous person, when it is brought about, can accomplish much. Elijah was a man with a nature like ours, and he prayed earnestly that it would not rain, and it did not rain on the earth for three years and six months. Then he prayed again, and the sky poured rain and the earth produced its fruit.

JAMES 5:16–18 NASB

Prayer is a powerful tool that God has given us, although we're not guaranteed to get exactly what we pray for. Through prayer, we join our hearts with God's. As we pray with the Spirit's leading, we lend our energies to the great, eternal song that is constantly going on in heaven, a prayer of blessing, praise, and gratitude that works to bring good even out of terrible situations. What an amazing privilege and honor God has given us!

Thank You, Lord, for allowing me to participate in Your kingdom through the power of prayer. I am so grateful for this privilege! Teach me to pray wisely, in line with Your Spirit.

Celebrating God

*GOD, your God, has been blessing you in your harvest and
in all your work, so make a day of it—really celebrate!*
DEUTERONOMY 16:15 MSG

Sometimes we need to set aside time to truly celebrate all that
God has done. We look at our work, and we realize how God has
blessed it. We see how He has been working in our families. We
know that we have been growing spiritually, and we are glad for
God's leading. There will inevitably be hard times again, times
full of pain and doubt and sorrow. But while the good times are
here, we need to express our praise and gratitude to God. Doing
so will strengthen us for whatever lies ahead.

I am so grateful, God, for all You have been
doing in my life. I want to celebrate You!

Manna

*"After all, our ancestors ate manna while they
journeyed through the wilderness! The Scriptures
say, 'Moses gave them bread from heaven to eat.'"*
JOHN 6:31 NLT

The Bible's stories can give us hope and strength for our lives. Although we're unlikely to be wandering hungry and thirsty in a literal desert, we do have times when we wonder how we're going to manage to get through the challenges of life. Perhaps we wonder where the money will come from to pay this month's bills, or maybe we doubt we have the emotional strength to keep going in a difficult situation. When times like these come, we can look at how God miraculously provided for His people in the wilderness. With joy and gratitude, we can claim that story as our own and wait to see how God will rescue us.

—————

I need some "manna," Lord. I've been wandering in this desert, and I'm hungry and desperate. I need Your help.

Always Present

"It was I who taught Ephraim to walk, taking them by the arms; but they did not realize it was I who healed them."

HOSEA 11:3 NIV

Sometimes we have reasons to be grateful to God that we never realize. We often fail to appreciate all the ways He has been working behind the scenes to bring about His will in our lives. From the moment we took our first toddling steps when we were babies, He was there beside us. As we learned our first words, He was there. When we went to kindergarten, He rode the bus beside us. When we learned to drive, when we left home for the first time, and through all the days of our lives, He has been there, leading and guiding even when we were completely unaware of His presence.

Lord, I am grateful for Your quiet,
helping presence in my life.

A Solid Foundation

A bad motive can't achieve a good end.
PROVERBS 17:20 MSG

We hear it all the time: "The end justifies the means." But that is not how it works in the kingdom of God. It's like trying to build a beautiful house on a shaky foundation. It just doesn't work. Sooner or later, the weak foundation will affect the rest of the house. True achievement is built on God's grace and love. That is the kind of foundation that holds solid no matter what.

Father, fill my heart with the longing and motivation to do Your work. Help me to build that work on the solid foundation of Your grace and love. Amen.

Without Condition

And my soul shall be joyful in the LORD:
it shall rejoice in his salvation.
PSALM 35:9 KJV

Knowing you're loved without condition sets you free. It invites you to abandon insecurity, relax, and enjoy being yourself. It encourages you to go ahead and try, because failure is simply a steep learning curve. God's acceptance of you is the key to this freedom. As you rest in God's absolute acceptance, you'll discover the confidence and courage you need to push beyond who you are today and become the woman you were created to be.

Lord, help me to live my life knowing You are pleased with me instead of trying to please others and following the social rules of the day. Help me to enjoy just being who You created me to be.

The Gratitude Song

Let everything that has breath praise the LORD.
PSALM 150:6 NIV

Take time to step outside sometime today. Listen to the wind in the trees, to the sound of birds; look for signs of insect life and watch for small, furry creatures going about their lives. Hear traffic going by and people calling. Now imagine that all these sights and sounds blend together into a chorus to God. This Bible verse calls on the entire living planet to lift up a song of praise and gratitude to the Lord. Everything that participates in respiration—plants and all manner of creatures, as well as human beings—is asked to take part in this song. Carry this song with you today.

Great Lord of love, may I sing out my gratitude to You.

Generosity and Blessing

No one is to show up in the Presence of God empty-handed; each man must bring as much as he can manage, giving generously in response to the blessings of God.

DEUTERONOMY 16:17 MSG

Again and again, the Bible tells us how we are to respond to God's blessings: we express our gratitude by giving generously back to God by giving to others. We never need to show up in God's presence empty-handed, because He always gives us plenty to pass along to others. We'll never be able to match His generosity, but we can allow ourselves to become free-flowing conduits of blessing, a bright river of generosity that streams from God through us to others around us. Our God has been so good to us, and we express our gratitude by passing along His goodness.

Generous Lord, make us more like You, constantly giving to everyone we meet.

Reach Out to Others

*Whoever has the gift of encouraging
others should encourage.*
ROMANS 12:8 NCV

Just as God encourages us, He wants us to encourage others. The word *encourage* comes from Latin words that mean "to put heart or inner strength into someone." When God encourages us, His heart reaches out to us and His strength becomes ours. As we rely on His grace, we are empowered to reach out to those around us, lending them our hearts and strength.

Lord, thank You for reaching out to me with Your heart and giving me Your strength. I pray that I would use that strength to encourage others. Amen.

Quiet Side of Love

Bless the LORD, O my soul, and forget not all his benefits.
PSALM 103:2 KJV

Kindness is a quiet side of love. It isn't showy, demanding center stage. It often serves in the background meeting needs, offering a word of encouragement or an impromptu hug. Sometimes kindness even travels under the name "anonymous." Likewise, the kindnesses God showers upon our lives often fall into the anonymous category. They're the coincidences, the unexpected pleasures, the little things that lift our hearts during a difficult day. How has God's kindness enriched your life this week?

———————————

Help me to see that as my fellow believers, the "body of Christ," show kindness to me, it is really You showering me with Your loving-kindness. I praise Your name!

Rewards

"There truly is a reward for those who live for God."
PSALM 58:11 NLT

No one can work endlessly without seeing any rewards. If we try, we get tired and burned out. That's why it's a good idea to stop now and then and notice the rewards of our labor. Maybe those rewards aren't exactly what we'd hoped for. Maybe we haven't earned as much money as we'd wished, maybe no one has noticed and praised us for our efforts the way we'd dreamed, and maybe the results we'd hoped for still haven't been realized. But if we look, we'll see that God has rewarded us in some way. As we take time to be grateful, we'll be encouraged to continue working.

Thank You, God, for rewarding my efforts.
Help me to keep working for You.

Praise Song

Praise the Lord from the heavens; praise him in the heights above. Praise him, all his angels; praise him, all his heavenly hosts. Praise him, sun and moon; praise him, all you shining stars. Praise him, you highest heavens and you waters above the skies. . . . Praise the Lord from the earth, you great sea creatures and all ocean depths, lightning and hail, snow and clouds, stormy winds that do his bidding, you mountains and all hills, fruit trees and all cedars, wild animals and all cattle, small creatures and flying birds, kings of the earth and all nations, you princes and all rulers on earth, young men and women, old men and children. Let them praise the name of the Lord.

PSALM 148:1–4, 7–13 NIV

Take a moment to sing this great song of praise and gratitude in your heart. Let it fill your thoughts. Continue to dwell on it throughout the day.

———

Teach me to daily sing Your song of praise, Lord.

Humble Work

*"God blesses those who are humble,
for they will inherit the whole earth."*
MATTHEW 5:5 NLT

Do you ever feel as though you spend your life doing laundry, cleaning up the kitchen, and vacuuming floors? These humble tasks that need to be done again and again can grow tedious. And yet even here, our God meets us. In the quiet, repetitive work of caring for a household, He blesses us, and we can be grateful for these ordinary chores. They are expressions of love to our family, and they mirror God's constant loving care that He bestows on each one of us. All work, no matter how humble, can be a source of blessing.

———

Thank You, God, for my home and family.
May the work I do to care for them reflect Your love.

Family Ties

Jesus, who makes people holy, and those who are made holy are from the same family. So he is not ashamed to call them his brothers and sisters.
HEBREWS 2:11 NCV

You and Jesus are family! Jesus, the one who made you whole and clean in God's sight, is your brother. Family ties connect you to Him and to all those with whom He is connected. In Christ, we find new connections with one another. By His grace, we are now kinfolk.

———————

Jesus, my brother, how grateful I am to be a part of Your holy family. Thank You for making me whole and clean and for inviting me into Your fold. Amen.

Reminders

*Let all that I am praise the LORD; with my whole heart,
I will praise his holy name. Let all that I am praise the
LORD; may I never forget the good things he does for
me. He forgives all my sins and heals all my diseases.
He redeems me from death and crowns me with love
and tender mercies. He fills my life with good things.*

PSALM 103:1–5 NLT

Verses like these are good to memorize. Write them on note
cards, and tape them to your walls or the visor of your car. Copy
them in your journal. Repeat them to yourself as you go about
your day or lie awake at night. Let them sink deep into your
being, for these verses are a wonderful reminder of all God has
done for us. He has forgiven us, healed us, redeemed us, crowned
us, filled our lives with good things, and renewed us. We have
so many reasons to be grateful!

Lord, thank You for Your constant generous grace.

Curses into Blessings

God, your God, refused to listen to Balaam but turned the curse into a blessing—how God, your God, loves you!
<small>Deuteronomy 23:5 MSG</small>

Sometimes we encounter people in life who wish us ill. They may actually curse us, or they may simply express their anger and resentment in ways that make us *feel* cursed. No one likes to find themselves in situations like these, and when we do, it's easy to become defensive. We don't have to return anger for anger, though, for God promises that, even now, we can be grateful for His ongoing blessing. Despite the words or emotions of others, He will turn things around and bring blessing out of curses. No human negativity can limit His grace and power.

God, when I'm tempted to get defensive, remind me that I don't need to, for You turn curses into blessings.

The End of Our Rope

"You're blessed when you're at the end of your rope.
With less of you there is more of God and his rule."
MATTHEW 5:3 MSG

The Bible is full of paradoxes like the one expressed in this verse.
We're blessed when we're at the end of our rope? How can that
be? When we've run out of resources, when our last nerve is
gone—that's when God blesses us? Yes, He does. And when we
find ourselves in those circumstances, we can actually be grateful.
When we have used up everything we have, then we are forced
to rely more fully on God. We can get out of His way so that He
has free rein to work in us and through us to accomplish His will.

Lord, when I'm at the end of my rope,
remind me that I can still praise You. Thank You
that You will always pick up where I leave off.

Leadership

*Thou leddest thy people like a flock by
the hand of Moses and Aaron.*
PSALM 77:20 KJV

Think of the leaders in your life. The list may include a boss, pastor, Bible study leader, mentor, chairperson, or the government officials helping steer the direction of the country you live in. The Bible encourages us to support and pray for our leaders. It doesn't add a disclaimer, saying this applies only if we like them, agree with them, or voted for them. How would God have you pray for your leaders today?

Lord, I lift up the leaders in my life to You.
From my local church body to the leaders of my
country, I ask Your will to be done in their lives.

Most Dear

*"You're blessed when you feel you've lost what
is most dear to you. Only then can you be
embraced by the One most dear to you."*
MATTHEW 5:4 MSG

Here's another paradox. How can we possibly be blessed when
we've lost what is most dear to us? And yet Jesus tells us that's
the case. As long as we're relying on other people for love and
approval, we'll never really come to know the full measure of
God's love and affirmation. Or maybe what's most dear to us is
our job. . .or our home. . .or a role, such as being a mother or a
grandmother. To lose one of those things would feel like a little
death. And yet God promises that should that happen, He will be
there. He will show us how dear we are to Him as He embraces
us with His loving arms.

When I lose what I value most, Lord, teach me to
turn to You. Thank You that Your love will never fail.

Just as We Are

*"You're blessed when you're content with just
who you are—no more, no less. That's the
moment you find yourselves proud owners
of everything that can't be bought."*
MATTHEW 5:5 MSG

Are you content with who you are? Do you find yourself wishing you were richer, smarter, thinner, more popular, more fashionable, more *something*? Most of us have times like that, but in this verse, Jesus is calling us to be content with ourselves exactly as we are right now. We don't have to wait to lose ten pounds or to get a promotion at work or to buy a new wardrobe. In God's eyes, we are absolutely fine just as we are. As we learn to accept God's perspective on us, we realize how much we really have. Instead of focusing on what we *don't* have, we overflow with gratitude for all He has given us.

Thank You, Lord, that You love me and
approve of me just as I am. May I learn
to see myself through Your eyes.

Cooperation

*"You're blessed when you can show people
how to cooperate instead of compete or fight.
That's when you discover who you really
are, and your place in God's family."*
MATTHEW 5:9 MSG

In today's world, we have plenty of opportunities to show others how to cooperate instead of argue and compete! Pick almost anything that's in the news, and you'll find that people have fierce and divided viewpoints on it. It's easy to be caught up in who's right (we are, of course!) and who's wrong (they are!), but that perspective just leads to more arguments, tension, and polarization. Instead, God wants us to discover that we belong to something far greater than any divided perspective on any issue. We are a member of God's family, and our job is to spread unity and understanding.

Help me, Jesus, to become a bridge between
points of view. May I be a calming influence
that points others away from their arguments
and helps them to focus instead on You.

Spreading Blessing

*All these blessings will come down on you
and spread out beyond you because you have
responded to the Voice of GOD, your God.*
DEUTERONOMY 28:2 MSG

The Bible is full of the voice of God. We may also hear His voice in nature. We may hear Him speaking to our hearts in a still, small voice. Or He may speak to us through other people or through the books we read. However we hear God talking to us, we are always called to respond. God wants to have a two-way conversation with us, a relationship that grows ever closer. When we do respond—with love, obedience, and gratitude—we are blessed. And when we are blessed, we have blessings to share with others. Blessings always spread!

Thank You, Lord, for speaking to me. Teach me to hear Your voice more clearly so that I may respond to You.

Back to God

*My dear brothers and sisters, always be willing
to listen and slow to speak. Do not become
angry easily, because anger will not help you
live the right kind of life God wants.*

JAMES 1:19–20 NCV

Our feelings are gifts from God, and we should never be ashamed of them. Instead, we need to offer them all back to God, both our joys and our frustrations. When we give God our anger, irritation, hurt feelings, and frustrations, we make room in our hearts to truly hear what others are saying.

Father, as uncomfortable as my feelings
can be sometimes, thank You for what they
teach me. Help me to trust You with all my
feelings so I can be a good listener. Amen.

The Perfect Friend

Lord, you are my God; I will exalt you and praise your name, for in perfect faithfulness you have done wonderful things, things planned long ago.
ISAIAH 25:1 NIV

Even our most faithful friends let us down sometimes. They're only human, after all, and sooner or later humans mess up, no matter how much they try not to. We can forgive our friends for being human (especially since we too are far from perfect!), but we can also be grateful that we have a friend who is perfectly faithful, who will never ever let us down, and who does wonderful things for us. Think about it: you have always been a part of God's plan. He has work prepared just for you, that only you can do, and He has plans to bless you in ways that only you can receive.

Lord my God, I'm so grateful that You
are my perfect friend who never fails me.
Thank You for all You have planned for my life.

Filled with the Spirit

Be filled with the Spirit, speaking to one another in psalms and hymns and spiritual songs, singing and making melody with your hearts to the Lord; always giving thanks for all things in the name of our Lord Jesus Christ to our God and Father.

EPHESIANS 5:18–20 NASB

Notice how Paul words this portion of his letter to the church at Ephesus: "Be filled with the Spirit." It's a command—something that's up to us. For the Spirit is always there, always willing; we just have to make room for Him. Paul is telling us how to do this: by talking publicly about our gratitude for all God has done, encouraging each other with scripture and spiritual songs while privately singing a song of thanksgiving in our deepest hearts. It's not complicated or hard to do. As we *always give thanks for all things*, the Spirit fills us.

Thank You, Holy Spirit, for all You are doing in my life. I am so grateful. Please fill me with You.

Failure

*Even though the fig trees have no blossoms,
and there are no grapes on the vines; even though
the olive crop fails, and the fields lie empty and
barren; even though the flocks die in the fields,
and the cattle barns are empty, yet I will rejoice in the
LORD! I will be joyful in the God of my salvation!*
HABAKKUK 3:17–18 NLT

Thanksgiving comes more easily when we see blessings everywhere we turn. Sometimes, though, it's hard to see the blessings. Although the spiritual world may tell a different story, the external, material world can seem pretty bleak. Sooner or later, we all have those times when everything we try seems to fail, when money is tight and our bank accounts are empty, when the physical blessings we hoped for fail to materialize. And yet even then, the prophet Habakkuk says, we can rejoice! Our salvation does not rely on this world. It relies on God.

When everything seems to be going wrong,
Lord, help me to praise You still.

New and Wonderful Things

Sing a new song to the LORD,
for He has done wonderful things.
PSALM 98:1 NASB

Just when we thought our lives would never change, when the same old problems would be following us the rest of our days, out of the blue, a breakthrough comes. God does something new and unexpected, something we never could have imagined. When that happens (and if it hasn't happened yet in your life, it will!), it's time for us to sing a new song of gratitude to God. He has blessed us in new ways, and we can find new ways to thank Him. Our God is so good to us, blessing us anew day after day, year after year.

Teach me to sing a new song to
You, Lord, for all the new and
wonderful things You do in my life.

Listen and Learn

*I will instruct thee and teach thee in the way which
thou shalt go: I will guide thee with mine eye.*
PSALM 32:8 KJV

To learn, you have to listen. Are you really listening to what God
is trying to teach you? Whether it's reading the Bible, listening
to a message at church, or receiving counsel from someone who
is farther down the road of faith than you happen to be, there is
always more to learn. Prepare your heart with prayer. Ask God
to help you clearly understand what you need to learn and then
act on what you hear.

Father God, please open my mind and
heart to understand what You want me
to learn. Give me wisdom and energy to
carry out the plans You have for me.

Redemption

Put your hope in the LORD, for with the LORD is
unfailing love and with him is full redemption.
PSALM 130:7 NIV

When God permits a redemption, or "buying back," of lost years and relationships, we get a black-and-white snapshot of the colorful mural of God's redemption of us in Christ. When we one day stand in His presence, we'll understand more clearly the marvelous scope of God's redeeming love. In ways we cannot begin to imagine. In broken relationships we thought could never be restored.

I praise You, Father, for Your awesome redemption.
Thank You that I've yet to see the scope of it all. Amen.

Our Confidence

Have no fear of sudden disaster or of the ruin that overtakes the wicked, for the LORD will be at your side and will keep your foot from being snared.
PROVERBS 3:25–26 NIV

Whether our loved ones are in harm's way daily or not, all of us live in a dangerous world. And while we should take physical precautions, our best preparation is spiritual. When we spend time with God and learn about His love for us and our families, we realize that He will give us His grace when we need it. He promises to never leave us, and the more we come to know His love, the more we will rest in that promise.

God, thank You that You promise Your peace to those who seek You. Help me to rest in Your love for my family and me.

Your Glorious Future

"No eye has seen, no ear has heard, and no mind has imagined what God has prepared for those who love him."
1 CORINTHIANS 2:9 NLT

God's promise for our future is so magnificent we can't even comprehend it. He has great plans for each of us, but we often become paralyzed by fear. Why? Because the past seems more comfortable. Because the future is uncertain. While God doesn't give us a map of what our future is like, He does promise that it will be more than we could ever ask or imagine. What steps of faith do you need to take today to accept God's glorious future for your life?

God, Your ways are not my ways and Your plans are too wonderful for me to even comprehend. Help me to never be satisfied with less than Your glorious plans for my life.

Smile, Smile, Smile

*"I will forget my complaint, I will change
my expression, and smile."*
JOB 9:27 NIV

Days may not go just as planned. We are all human, and we can't always control our circumstances. What we can control, however, is our attitude. Remember each day that you are a representative of Jesus Christ. As a Christian and a woman, it is important to model a godly attitude at all times. Even a small look or smile can help show others the love of God. Just because we don't feel like having a good attitude doesn't mean we shouldn't try. God tells us to praise Him always—in good times and in bad. Let that praise show on your face today.

Lord, I know I can choose my attitude. Help me to
show Your love to others by having a positive attitude
each day. Let Your glory show on my face. Amen.

Our Companion

Our LORD, you are the friend of your worshipers,
and you make an agreement with all of us.
PSALM 25:14 CEV

God is our friend. He is our companion through life's journey.
He is the one who always understands us; and no matter what
we do, He always accepts us and loves us. What better agreement
could we have with anyone than what we have with God?

Father, thank You for being my friend,
my companion, my comfort. Thank You for
the everlasting covenant You have made with
me. I am grateful to be Your child. Amen.

Prayer

Jesus often withdrew to lonely places and prayed.
LUKE 5:16 NIV

Jesus is our perfect role model. If He withdrew often to pray, shouldn't we? Do we think we can continually give to others without getting replenished ourselves? Make prayer a priority. Recognize that the Lord must daily fill your cup so that you will have something to give. Set aside a specific time, a specific place. Start slow. Give Him five minutes every day. As you are faithful, your relationship with Him will grow. Over time you will crave the time spent together as He fills your cup to overflowing. Follow Jesus' example and pray!

Dear Lord, help me set aside time to pray each day. Please fill my cup so that I can share with others what You have given me. Amen.

Sweating the Small Stuff

Blessed are all who fear the LORD, who walk in obedience to him. You will eat the fruit of your labor; blessings and prosperity will be yours.
PSALM 128:1–2 NIV

The Lord showers us with many blessings each day—family, friends, education, job, good health, and a beautiful earth. But despite the gifts He gives, it's easy to get bogged down in the little things that go wrong. We're all human, and we sometimes focus on all the negatives rather than the positives in life. Next time you're feeling that "woe is me" attitude, remember that you are a child of God. Spend some time counting all the wonderful blessings that come from the Lord rather than the headaches from this earth.

Father, thank You that I am Your child.
Remind me each day to count the many
blessings You shower upon me rather than
focusing on the negatives of this world. Amen.

Seasons of Change

*The Spirit of God, who raised Jesus from the dead,
lives in you. And just as God raised Christ Jesus
from the dead, he will give life to your mortal
bodies by this same Spirit living within you.*
ROMANS 8:11 NLT

Change can be exciting or fearsome. Changing a habit or moving beyond your comfort zone can leave you feeling out of control. The power of God that formed the world, brought the dry land above the waters of the sea, and raised Jesus from the dead is alive and active today. Imagine what it takes to overcome the natural laws of gravity to put the earth and seas in place. Imagine the power to bring the dead to life again. That same power is available to work out the details of your life.

Lord, I want to grow and fulfill all You've
destined me to be. Help me to accept change
and depend on Your strength to make the
changes I need in my life today. Amen.

Our Rock and Savior

"The LORD lives! Praise be to my Rock!
Exalted be my God, the Rock, my Savior!"
2 SAMUEL 22:47 NIV

Throughout the psalms, we read that David not only worshipped and praised God, he also complained to Him, was honest with God about what he was feeling, and even admitted to being angry at God. Perhaps the most amazing thing about David, though, was his constant devotion and reliance on his Creator. Even though David is the powerful king of Israel, he praises God in 2 Samuel 22:47, calling Him his rock and Savior. David knew that God was alive, and he also knew that he needed Him more than anything else in the world. It's the same for us today!

Dear Lord, You are my rock and my Savior.
You are alive, and I praise You as God above all
else. Thank You for Your love and power. Amen.

Godly Counsel

The mouth of the righteous speaketh wisdom,
and his tongue talketh of judgment.
PSALM 37:30 KJV

Want to run a marathon? Talk to those who've run one. They know how to train, which shoes to buy, and what to expect when the big day arrives. The same is true if you want to go the distance with God. When you meet people who have followed God for many years, ask questions. Discover what they've learned, where they've struggled, and how they study the Bible. You may gain new friends as well as godly counsel.

Lord, please bring people into my life who can offer godly wisdom from a lifetime of trusting You. Prepare my heart to accept their wisdom.

Hold His Hand

*"For I am the LORD your God who takes hold of your
right hand and says to you, Do not fear; I will help you."*
ISAIAH 41:13 NIV

God desires to help us. When we walk through life hand in hand
with God, we can face anything. His love covers us. His presence
is our guard. We can do all things through Christ because we are
given His strength. Do you feel as though you're walking through
life alone? Do not fear. Are you in need of love, protection, courage, and strength? Reach out your hand. Allow Jesus to take hold
of it. Receive His love and protection. Bask in His courage and
strength. Take hold of His hand!

Dear Lord, thank You that I do not have to fear.
You will help me by taking my hand. Amen.

Truth

"You will know the truth, and the truth will set you free."
JOHN 8:32 NLT

What lies do you believe about yourself? How might those lies be preventing you from experiencing God's plan for *your* life? The next time you're tempted to believe a lie, write it down. Then find a scripture passage that speaks truth over the situation. Write that scripture verse across the lie. Commit the truth to memory. Over time God's Word will transform your thinking, and you'll begin to believe the truth. Then something amazing will happen—you'll be set free.

Father, thank You for the truth Your Word speaks about my life. Open my eyes to the truth and help me to believe it. Amen.

Never Lost for Long

For "whoever calls on the name
of the LORD shall be saved."
ROMANS 10:13 NKJV

You call out to God, but maybe for a little while you don't hear anything. You may have to listen intently for a while, but eventually you are reassured by His voice. When He calls your name, you know you are safe. You may have to take a few steps in the dark, but by moving toward Him, you eventually see clearly. A light comes on in your heart, and you recognize where you are and what you need to do to get back on the path God has set before you.

Heavenly Father, help me to stay focused on
You. Show me how to remove distractions from
my life so I can stay close to You. Amen.

A Valuable Deposit

*He anointed us, set his seal of ownership
on us, and put his Spirit in our hearts as a
deposit, guaranteeing what is to come.*
2 CORINTHIANS 1:21–22 NIV

When we commit our lives to Christ, He doesn't let us flail around in this mixed-up world without any help. We have the deposit of the Holy Spirit with us all the time, and He also gives us His Word and the help of other Christians to keep us strong in the Lord. So whenever you feel alone or overwhelmed with life, remember that God has anointed you, set His seal upon you, and deposited the Holy Spirit right inside your heart. That is the most valuable deposit of all!

Dear Lord, thank You for depositing
Your Holy Spirit in my heart to lead and
guide me. Help me to listen. Amen.

The Next Oasis

The LORD will always guide you and provide good things to eat when you are in the desert. He will make you healthy. You will be like a garden that has plenty of water or like a stream that never runs dry.
ISAIAH 58:11 CEV

God wants you to be healthy—not just physically but emotionally, intellectually, and spiritually as well. He wants to fill your life full of all the things you truly need. The life He wants for you is not dry, empty, and barren. It is lush and full of delicious things to nourish you. We all have to cross life's deserts sometimes, but even then God will supply what you need to reach the next oasis He has waiting.

Lord, this life can feel like an incredibly long journey, especially when I am in the desert. Sustain and strengthen me with the promises of Your Word. Amen.

Wonderful Things

Everything God made is waiting with excitement
for God to show his children's glory completely.
ROMANS 8:19 NCV

Some days it's hard to feel very optimistic. We listen to the evening news and hear story after story about natural disasters and human greed. God doesn't want us to be ostriches, hiding our heads in the sand, refusing to acknowledge what's going on in the world. But He also wants us to believe that the future is full of wonderful things He has planned. The whole world is holding its breath, waiting for God's wonderful grace to reveal itself.

God, I cannot even begin to comprehend the
riches You have in store for us, Your children.
When I am discouraged, lift my head and
remind me of Your promise. Amen.

Fear and Dread

What I feared has come upon me;
what I dreaded has happened to me.
JOB 3:25 NIV

Do we have a secret fear or dread? God knew Job's secret fears but still called him "blameless and upright" (Job 1:8 NIV). God doesn't withhold His love if we harbor unspoken dread. He doesn't love us any less because of secret anxieties. The Lord "is like a father to his children. . .he remembers we are only dust" (Psalm 103:13–14 NLT). God never condemned Job (and He'll never condemn us) for private fears. He encourages us, as He did Job, to trust Him. He alone retains control over all creation and all circumstances (Job 38–41).

Father, please stay beside me when what
I dread most comes to me. Amen.

Choices

I place before you Life and Death, Blessing and Curse.
Choose life so that you and your children will live.
And love GOD, your God, listening obediently to
him, firmly embracing him. Oh yes, he is life itself.
DEUTERONOMY 30:19–20 MSG

God gives us choices in life. We can choose ways of life and blessing or choose to walk on paths leading to destruction and pain. God doesn't punish us for our choices, but He doesn't necessarily step in and save us from their consequences. It's up to us to pick which roads we want to follow. But why would we want to choose destruction and pain when God longs to lead us into the fullness of life? He yearns to show us a life that will fill our hearts with the deepest gratitude possible. All we have to do is follow Him.

God of grace, thank You for leading me to life.
Give me strength, courage, and wisdom so that I always
follow You. I choose Your path, Lord. I choose You.

Light in the Dark

The light shines in the darkness,
and the darkness has not overcome it.
JOHN 1:5 NIV

Jesus said in John 12:46 (NIV), "I have come into the world as a light, so that no one who believes in me should stay in darkness." He also promised that He is always with us. Because we have Him, we have light. If we fail to perceive it, if we seem to be living in darkness, perhaps we have turned our backs to the light of His countenance. Maybe we are covering our eyes with the cares of this world. Clouds of sin may be darkening our lives, but He has not left us. He promises us that in following Him, we will not walk in darkness but have the light of life.

Lord Jesus, show me my blind spots.
Where am I covering my eyes or walking away
from You? Turn me back to You, the light of life.

Jumping Hurdles

God's way is perfect. All the LORD's promises prove true.
PSALM 18:30 NLT

Maybe there are times when you just don't think you can take one more disappointment or hurt. That's the perfect time to draw strength from God and His Word. Meditate on encouraging scriptures, or play a song that you know strengthens your heart and mind. Ask God to infuse you with His strength, and you'll find the power to take another step and another until you find yourself on the other side of that challenge you're facing today.

God, give me strength each day to face the obstacles I am to overcome. I am thankful that I don't have to face them alone. Amen.

Good for You!

*A happy heart is like good medicine,
but a broken spirit drains your strength.*
PROVERBS 17:22 NCV

God longs to make you happy. He knows that happiness is good for you. Mentally and physically, you function better when you are happy. Discouragement and sadness sap your strength. It's like trying to work while carrying a heavy load on your back: it slows you down and makes everything harder. Let God heal the breaks in your spirit. His grace can make you strong and happy.

Father, I know the heaviness of a broken spirit.
Heal me and help me carry my burdens. Remind me of
the reasons I have to be grateful and happy. Amen.

God-Honoring Life

So teach us to number our days,
that we may apply our hearts unto wisdom.
PSALM 90:12 KJV

Want to live life in a way that honors God? There are so many options it's hard to know what to do. But in Matthew 22:37–39, Jesus sums up the purpose of life by saying we're to love God and love others. Prayerfully weighing the choices before us against these two commands can help us make wise decisions. We don't know how long our lives will be, but with love as our goal, we're certain to use our time well.

Lord, let my life goals line up with Your goals
for me—to love You and to love others well.
May I make choices based on those goals alone.

My Future Is in Your Hands

The LORD says, "I will guide you along the best pathway
for your life. I will advise you and watch over you."
PSALM 32:8 NLT

Are plans running wild in your head? Remember that the Lord is watching over you, and He is there to guide you. He wants you to seek Him. Don't try to make your dreams happen by yourself. Get on your knees and ask Him to direct your plans each morning. Don't be afraid to put your future in His hands!

Father, thank You for always being faithful to me.
Continue to watch over me and direct my path. Amen.

Wells of Salvation

With joy you will draw water from the wells of salvation.
ISAIAH 12:3 NIV

Sometimes we talk as though salvation in Jesus is a thing that happens once and is done. In one sense, this may be true, but in another sense, salvation is an ongoing thing, something that never ends. God has put "wells of salvation"—sources of life and refreshment—throughout our lives. The Hebrew word translated "salvation" in this verse meant a bunch of things: welfare, prosperity, victory, help, deliverance, health. All these things God has promised to give us, and we find them in many "wells"—in our friends and family, through prayer, through scripture, through time alone, through the beauty of nature. As we draw from them, we will be filled with joy.

Thank You, Lord, for Your deep wells of
salvation springing up in my life. I am so
grateful for all the ways You help me,
save me, deliver me, and make me healthy.

Breathing

In certain ways we are weak, but the Spirit is here to help us. For example, when we don't know what to pray for, the Spirit prays for us in ways that cannot be put into words.
ROMANS 8:26 CEV

The Holy Spirit is the wind that blows through our world, breathing grace and life into everything that exists. He will breathe through you as you open yourself to Him. We need not worry about our own weakness or mistakes, for the Spirit will make up for them. His creative power will pray through us, work through us, and love through us.

Holy Spirit, thank You for interceding on my behalf, for breathing grace and life into me. Even through my weakness, thank You for Your power that carries my very breath to God. Amen.

Learn Contentment

*I am not saying this because I am in need, for I have
learned to be content whatever the circumstances.*
PHILIPPIANS 4:11 NIV

Contentment is learned and cultivated. It is an attitude of the
heart. It has nothing to do with material possessions or life's
circumstances. It has everything to do with being in the center
of God's will and knowing it. Contentment means finding rest
and peace in God's presence—nothing more, nothing less. It is
trusting that God will meet all your needs. May we learn to say
confidently, "The Lord is my shepherd, I shall not want." That is
the secret of contentment.

Dear Lord, teach me how to be content in You,
knowing that You will provide all that I need. Amen.

Joyful Noise

Make a joyful noise unto the LORD, all the earth:
make a loud noise, and rejoice, and sing praise.
PSALM 98:4 KJV

The entire earth sings a song of gratitude to the Lord, and the Bible asks us humans to join in. Don't be quiet about it, says the scripture. Don't be shy. Shout out loud. Bang drums. Sing at the top of your lungs. Stomp your feet. God has done so much for us. His beauty, kindness, and love are everywhere we turn. Back in the fourteenth century, a German clergyman named Meister Eckhart said, "If the only prayer you ever said was 'thank You,' it would be enough." So make your "thank You" a joyful noise that fills your life.

Lord, I thank You for all You have done for
me. I thank You for the beauties of the earth,
for the pleasures of friendship and family,
and most of all, for Jesus, who shows me You.

Wait and Praise

I will wait continually, and will praise
You yet more and more.
PSALM 71:14 NASB

In Hebrew, the word *praise* had to do with singing, thanksgiving, and adoration. This verse connects praise to waiting. We can look at life with a gloomy outlook, expecting bad things to happen. Or we can be confident that even though bad things may happen, God is still in charge. To wait means to look foward to what God is doing. We're patient in the midst of trouble. We anticipate the day, however distant, when we will see clearly what God has planned all along. And as we cultivate this attitude, we'll find it easier and easier to praise God.

———————

I praise You, God. I adore You. I give You thanks for I know You are working out Your perfect will.

Heavenly Appreciation

*God is not unjust; he will not forget your work
and the love you have shown him as you have
helped his people and continue to help them.*
HEBREWS 6:10 NIV

Sometimes it seems our hard work is ignored. When our work for Christ seems to go unnoticed by our church family, we can be assured that God sees our hard work and appreciates it. We may not receive the "church member of the month" award, but our love for our brothers and sisters in Christ and our work on their behalf is not overlooked by God. The author of Hebrews assures us that God is not unjust—our reward is in heaven.

Dear Lord, You are a God of love and justice.
Even when I do not receive the notice of those around
me, help me to serve You out of my love for You. Amen.

Smoothing Rough Edges

*Behold, how good and how pleasant it is for
brethren to dwell together in unity!*
PSALM 133:1 KJV

The feel of sandpaper rubbing against unfinished wood isn't pleasant. Neither is the experience of two good friends rubbing each other the wrong way. But when friends are authentic and vulnerable with each other, it's bound to happen—and that's a good thing. It helps bring our weaknesses to light. Helping smooth out one another's rough edges is part of God's plan. If friendship hits a rough patch, stay close and work through the friction. Let love help you grow.

Lord, please allow my friends and me to
sharpen one another. Let love guide all of our
thoughts and actions toward each other as we
show grace and truth in our friendships.

Extraordinary Treasures

*What man is he that desireth life, and loveth
many days, that he may see good?*
PSALM 34:12 KJV

God is amazingly creative and incomparably loving. Having
someone like that design a plan for your life is an exciting pros-
pect. God promises there are good things ahead for you. That
promise is enough to make each morning feel like a chest filled
with treasure just waiting to be opened. Greet each new day
with expectation. Invite God to join you in your search for the
extraordinary treasures He's scattered throughout even the most
ordinary of days.

Before my feet hit the ground, remind me
that You are with me Lord Jesus. Help me
to see Your blessings in each new day.

Of Him, through Him, to Him

For of him, and through him, and to him,
are all things: to whom be glory for ever.
ROMANS 11:36 KJV

Everywhere we turn, God is there. Nothing is too small or ordinary for His presence. As this verse tells us, everything is of God, everything comes to us through God, and everything is on its way to God. We often cannot see this constant process with our earthly eyes, and yet the Bible tells us it is a reality that exists all around us. Every ordinary piece of our life—computers, cell phones, commutes to work, social media, children's laughter, friends' smiles, family meals, household chores, glorious sunsets, sleepless nights, morning coffee—all of it is immersed in God. All of it is reason to give Him thanks and praise.

God, thank You for all the ordinary pieces of
my life. Thank You that all things are in You.

Creation

*Blessed be your glorious name, exalted above all blessing
and praise! You're the one, GOD, you alone; you made the
heavens, the heavens of heavens, and all angels; the earth
and everything on it, the seas and everything in them;
you keep them all alive; heaven's angels worship you!*

NEHEMIAH 9:5–6 MSG

Again and again, the Bible reminds us that praise and thanksgiving are woven throughout the universe. From the earth that shelters countless wonderful creatures, to the vast seas teeming with life, to the far reaches of outer space, to the angels of heaven, all creation not only was made by God but continues to rely on Him for life. He sustains the tiny creatures found in soil and water as much as He does the angels, as much as He does us. All of us, from microbes to angelic hosts, rely on God for life.

I praise You, Lord of life, for Your amazing creation.

Spirit and Truth

"But the time is coming—indeed it's here now—when true worshipers will worship the Father in spirit and in truth."
JOHN 4:23 NLT

God is everywhere all the time, and He doesn't just want to be worshipped at church. You can worship God on your way to work, during class, as you clean your house, and while you pay your bills. Worship is about living your life in a way that is pleasing to the Lord and seeking Him first in all things. Paying your bills? Ask God how He wants you to spend your money. That is pleasing to Him, and that is worship. In the middle of class? Be respectful of your professors, and use the brain God gave you to complete your studies. If you are living your everyday life to please God, that is worship!

Father, help me to live my life in ways that please You. Let my focus be on worshipping You in everything I do. Amen.

Changing Our Perspective

*Turn my eyes away from worthless things;
preserve my life according to your word.*
PSALM 119:37 NIV

The book of Psalms offers hundreds of verses that can easily become sentence prayers. "Turn my eyes away from worthless things" whispered before heading out to shop, turning on the television, or picking up a magazine can turn those experiences into opportunities to see God's hand at work in our lives. He can change our perspective. He will show us what has value for us. He can even change our appetites, causing us to desire the very things He wants for us. When we pray this prayer, we are asking God to show us what He wants for us. He knows us and loves us more than we know and love ourselves. We can trust His love and goodness to provide for our needs.

Father, imprint this scripture in my mind today.
In moments of need, help me remember to pray
this prayer and to relinquish my desires to You.

An Attitude

*God proves to be good to the man who passionately
waits, to the woman who diligently seeks. It's a good
thing to quietly hope, quietly hope for help from God.*
LAMENTATIONS 3:25 MSG

Hope is an attitude not an emotion. It means putting our whole
hearts into relying on God. It means keeping our eyes focused
on Him no matter what, waiting for Him to reveal Himself in
our lives. God never disappoints those who passionately wait for
His help, who diligently seek His grace.

God, help me to passionately wait and diligently
seek. Help me not to be frantic, but to quietly hope
for the help that is sure to come from You. Amen.

Grace in Return

"Then those 'sheep' are going to say, 'Master, what are you talking about? When did we ever see you hungry and feed you, thirsty and give you a drink? . . .' Then the King will say, 'I'm telling the solemn truth: Whenever you did one of these things to someone overlooked or ignored, that was me—you did it to me.'"
MATTHEW 25:37–40 MSG

If Christ were sitting on our doorstep, lonely, tired, and hungry, what would we do? Hopefully, we would throw the door wide open and welcome Him into our home. But the truth is we're given the opportunity to offer our hospitality to Jesus each time we're faced with a person in need. His grace reaches out to us through those who feel misunderstood and overlooked, and He wants us to offer that same grace in return.

Jesus, open my eyes to the hungry and thirsty all around me. Whether their hunger is spiritual, physical, or both, help me give them Your grace. Amen.

Seeds

Thy wife shall be as a fruitful vine by the sides of thine house: thy children like olive plants round about thy table.

PSALM 128:3 KJV

There are many ways to be fruitful. One way is through relationships. Whether it's with family, friends, neighbors, church members, or coworkers, the things you say and do can be buds that blossom into something beautiful. Who will you spend time with today? Each encounter is an opportunity to plant a seed. Will it be a seed of encouragement, grace, faith, comfort, or...? Ask God to help you know the type of seed others need.

Father, please bring people into my life who need encouragement from me. I also ask that You would put me on the path of those who can encourage me as well. Help me know what seeds need to be sown.

Freely Given

*Out of sheer generosity he put us in right standing
with himself. A pure gift. He got us out of the mess
we're in and restored us to where he always wanted
us to be. And he did it by means of Jesus Christ.*

ROMANS 3:24 MSG

How kind God has been to us! He brought us close to Himself. He
reached down and picked us up out of our messy lives. He healed
us so we could be the people we were always meant to be. That
is what grace is: a gift we never deserved, freely given out of love.

Oh kind, gracious, and generous heavenly
Father, thank You for the gift of Your Son,
for pulling me out of the mess and restoring
me to a right relationship with You. Amen.

Connected

Turn thee unto me, and have mercy upon me; for I am desolate and afflicted.
PSALM 25:16 KJV

In Genesis we read about creation. God declared everything He created "good," with one exception. God said it was not good for Adam to be alone. God designed people to be in relationships with each other and with Him. When you're feeling lonely, God agrees: it's not good. Ask God to bring a new friend your way and help you connect more deeply with those already in your life. But for right now, invite God to meet your deepest need.

Heavenly Father, please bring friends into my life who can become good and healthy members of my family. I trust You to meet my need for healthy, thriving relationships.

God as He Really Is

The LORD is compassionate and gracious, slow to anger,
abounding in love. . . . He does not treat us as our
sins deserve or repay us according to our iniquities.
PSALM 103:8, 10 NIV

Our attitude toward God can influence the way we handle what He has given us. Some people perceive God as a harsh and angry judge, impatiently tapping His foot, saying, "When will you ever get it right?" People who see God this way can become paralyzed by an unhealthy fear of Him. However, the Bible paints a very different picture of God. Psalm 103 says He is gracious and compassionate, that He does not treat us as our sins deserve. What difference can it make in your life to know that you serve a loving God who is longing to be gracious to you?

Lord, thank You for Your compassion, Your grace,
and Your mercy. Help me to see You as You really are.

Behind the Scenes

*My mouth shall tell of Your righteousness
and of Your salvation all day long.*
PSALM 71:15 NASB

We don't know all the ways that God has come to our rescue, all the ways He has blessed us with life and well-being, for He is constantly working behind the scenes on our behalf. His care for us is ongoing, never ending, and so our expression of gratitude also should be ongoing and never ending. All day long, our thoughts and conversation (our inner words and outer words) should dwell on God's goodness. Gratitude should be the constant background noise of our lives.

You are so good to me, God. I'm incapable of counting all the ways You have blessed me.

The Number Seven

Seven times a day I praise you for your righteous laws.
PSALM 119:164 NIV

The number seven in the Bible has special significance. It is the number of completeness and perfection (both physical and spiritual), and it is connected to God's creation of the world in seven days. So when the psalmist says that he praises God seven times a day, he may mean that literally, but he also means, symbolically, that praise and thanksgiving are necessary for the completion of his day. Without thanksgiving, the day would be incomplete. Gratitude expressed in praise is what gives our life meaning; it is what fulfills our days.

Lord, remind me today to say thank
You to You at least seven times!

Act in Love

Let all that you do be done in love.
1 CORINTHIANS 16:14 NRSV

Because love is not merely an emotion, it needs to become real through action. We grow in love as we act in love. Some days the emotion may overwhelm us; other days we may feel nothing at all. But if we express our love while making meals, driving the car, talking to our families, or cleaning the house, God's love will flow through us to the world around us, and we will see His grace at work.

Father, when I feel love, it's easy to show it. But the feelings are not always there. Help me to find ways to obediently express Your love through all my actions. Amen.

The Harvest

And let the beauty of the LORD our God be upon us: and establish thou the work of our hands upon us; yea, the work of our hands establish thou it.

PSALM 90:17 KJV

If you plant an apple tree, you probably hope to enjoy its fruit someday. But hoping, and even praying, won't guarantee a good harvest. A fruit tree needs to be watered, pruned, and protected from bugs, frost, and hail. It needs God's gift of life and your loving care. The same is true for any project you're working on. Work hard, pray hard, and wait patiently for God's good timing. Then, when harvesttime arrives, remember to give thanks.

Please give me eyes to see Your hands at work all around me, Creator God. I want to be in on the work You are doing in my little portion of the world.

Living a Complete Life

It is a good thing to receive wealth from
God and the good health to enjoy it.
ECCLESIASTES 5:19 NLT

God has promised to supply all your needs, but it takes action on your part. Seeking wisdom for your situation and asking God to direct you will help you find a well-balanced life that will produce success coupled with the health to enjoy it. It may be as simple as realizing a vacation is exactly what you need, instead of working throughout the year and taking your vacation in cash to pay for new bedroom furniture. Know when to press forward and when to stop and enjoy the life God has given you for His good pleasure—and yours!

Lord, I ask for Your wisdom to help me balance my life so I can be complete in every area of my life. Amen.

Faith and Action

And I keep praying that this faith we hold in common keeps showing up in the good things we do, and that people recognize Christ in all of it.
PHILEMON 6 MSG

Our actions and reactions are a powerful gauge of how serious we are about our faith. When others wrong us, do we refuse to forgive and risk misrepresenting Christ, or do we freely offer forgiveness as an expression of our faith? God calls us to faith and forgiveness in Christ Jesus so that Christians and non-Christians alike will see our good deeds and praise God.

Dear Lord, please let me remember that people look to me for a glimpse of You. Let my actions always reflect my faith in You. Amen.

Quiet Grace

Patient persistence pierces through indifference;
gentle speech breaks down rigid defenses.
PROVERBS 25:15 MSG

When we're in the midst of an argument, we often become fixated on winning. We turn conflicts into power struggles, and we want to come out the victor. By sheer force, if necessary, we want to shape people to our will. But that is not the way God treats us. His grace is gentle and patient rather than loud and forceful. We need to follow His example and let His quiet grace speak through us in His timing rather than ours.

Father, thank You for the gentleness of Your grace. Give me a spirit of patient persistence. Instill my words with gentleness. May I always value relationships over being right. Amen.

God's Presence

Unto thee, O my strength, will I sing: for God is my defence, and the God of my mercy.
PSALM 59:17 KJV

When you're feeling lonely, picture God beside you in the room. Talk to Him the way you would a dear friend. If praying aloud feels awkward, journal or write God a love note that you can tuck in your Bible. Read the book of Psalms. See what other people had to say to God when they felt the way you do right now. Remember, God is with you, whether you're aware of His presence or not.

I ask again, Lord, that You open my eyes to spiritual things. I feel alone, and I want to know that You are near. Please show Yourself to me.

Holding the Line

When I said, "My foot is slipping," your unfailing love, Lord, supported me. When anxiety was great within me, your consolation brought me joy.
PSALM 94:18–19 NIV

Often we may feel that our feet are slipping in life. We lose our grip. Anxiety becomes a sleep-robber, headache-giver, and joy-squelcher. Fear takes over our hearts. All we can think is, *Just get me out of here!* But we must remember who is anchoring our life. God's powerful grip secures us even in the most difficult times. He comforts us with His loving presence that defies understanding. He provides wisdom to guide our steps through life's toughest challenges. We can rest assured that His support is steady, reliable, and motivated by His love for us.

Jesus, my rock and fortress, thank You that Your strength is made available to me. Steady me with the surety of Your love. Replace my anxiety with peace and joy, reflecting a life that's secured by the Almighty. Amen.

Intergenerational Gratitude

*One generation will declare Your works to the
next and will proclaim Your mighty acts.*
PSALM 145:4 HCSB

We pass along to our children and grandchildren many things,
some of them intentional, some not. Some things we may wish
we had kept to ourselves, not burdening another generation
with them.

Thanksgiving could be part of our legacy to the next generation. As we make it our daily, moment-by-moment habit, the
children in our lives will notice. Consciously or unconsciously,
they will absorb this way of thinking and acting. The more we talk
about God and express our gratitude for all His blessings, the more
likely the next generations will adopt a lifestyle of thanksgiving.

Lord, I want to leave behind a legacy of
gratitude. Teach me to be thankful continually.

Nothing for Granted

You lifted him high and bright as a cumulus cloud,
then dressed him in rainbow colors. You pile blessings
on him; you make him glad when you smile.
PSALM 21:6 MSG

To be grateful is to recognize God's love and beauty everywhere we turn. Every breath we breathe is a gift of His love; every moment of our lives is full of His blessing. He lifts us up and makes us shine. His smile fills us with joy. When we practice gratitude, we take absolutely nothing for granted. We respond to each of life's smallest delights. Gratitude wakes us up again and again to new wonders in the world around us. As author Thomas Merton wrote, "The grateful person knows that God is good, not by hearsay but by experience. And that is what makes all the difference."

Thank You, Lord, for piling so many blessings
on me. May I take none of them for granted.

A Spiritual Can Opener

*It is good to give thanks to the LORD and to
sing praises to Your name, Most High.*
PSALM 92:1 NASB

"Gratitude," said the ancient Roman philosopher Cicero, "is not only the greatest of virtues, but the parent of all others." The Bible reinforces this idea, speaking again and again of thanks, praise, and gratefulness. You might say that gratitude is like a spiritual can opener that opens our hearts to God. As our hearts open, other blessings can come into us, including the blessing of the Holy Spirit's presence within us. So make gratitude a habit. Practice it daily. May it fill your thoughts and prayers so that God in turn can bless you even more richly.

Thank You, Lord. I am so grateful to
You for all You have done for me!

Constant Grace

For Jesus doesn't change—yesterday,
today, tomorrow, he's always totally himself.
HEBREWS 13:8 MSG

As human beings, we live in the stream of time. Sometimes all the changes time brings terrify us; sometimes they fill us with joy and excitement. Either way, we can cling to the still point that lies in the middle of our changing world: Jesus Christ, who never changes. His constant grace leads us through all life's changes, and one day it will bring us to our home in heaven, beyond time, where we will be like Him.

Jesus, how grateful I am that You stay the same. Yesterday, today, and forever, I can count on You to remain firm and steadfast, no matter how much change life brings. Amen.

A Wise Woman

*Don't jump to conclusions—there may be a perfectly
good explanation for what you just saw.*
PROVERBS 25:8 MSG

You cry at movies; your sister doesn't. Your husband shares openly
with anyone he meets; you prefer to take time getting to know
someone first. You enjoy working alone; your boss works best
on a team. Your mother gives instant solutions; you like mulling
over the options. It's easy to jump to conclusions when another
person doesn't think or act as you do. But when you suspend
judgment of the differing ideas and opinions of others, you're a
wise—and gracious—woman.

Heavenly Father, help me to stop my constant judging.
You've created all of us different for Your purposes.
Fill me with Your love and graciousness toward others.

Standing Firm

I. . .didn't dodge their insults, faced them as they spit in my face. And the Master, GOD, stays right there and helps me, so I'm not disgraced. Therefore I set my face like flint, confident that I'll never regret this. My champion is right here. Let's take our stand together!

ISAIAH 50:6–8 MSG

Isaiah reminds us that we are not alone in our battles, even when everyone is against us and we feel outnumbered and outmaneuvered. But remember, your champion, God, is right there, saying, "I am not leaving you! We are sticking this out together. You can put your chin up confidently, knowing that I, the sustainer, am on your side. Let's take our stand together!"

Lord, boldly stand beside me. May the strength of Your arms gird me as I take a stand for You. Lift my chin today; give me confidence to face opposition, knowing You are right there with me. Amen.

Secure in Truth

*Throw off your old sinful nature and your former
way of life, which is corrupted by lust and deception.
Instead, let the Spirit renew your thoughts and
attitudes. Put on your new nature, created to
be like God—truly righteous and holy.*

EPHESIANS 4:22–24 NLT

In Christ, we have a new mindset—fresh thinking. We know we
are loved and treasured. The very God who spoke the universe
into existence loved us enough to leave heaven and live in this
imperfect world so He could save us from eternity in the hell we
so deserved. Talk about significance! The delusions of this world
fall away in light of who He is and what He has done for love
of us. Our daily intake of His Word secures us in those truths.

Christ, rid me of my old way of thinking.
Put the new mindset within me to see daily the
lies I fall for. Help me to walk in rightness and
holiness, reflecting You in all I am. Amen.

Great Is His Love

*For as the heaven is high above the earth,
so great is his mercy toward them that fear him.*
PSALM 103:11 KJV

It's hard to grasp how deeply God cares for us, because our first-hand experience of love comes from relationships with imperfect people. But God's love is different. With God, we need never fear condemnation, misunderstanding, or rejection. He completely understands what we say and how we feel, and He loves us without condition. Since God is never fickle or self-centered, we can risk opening every part of our lives to Him. We can risk returning the love He so freely gives.

I love You, heavenly Father. I want to honor
You with my life and share every part of my
heart with You. I seek You with all my heart.

Splashes

To get wisdom is to love oneself;
to keep understanding is to prosper.
PROVERBS 19:8 NRSV

If you can accept yourself, you will probably be able to more readily accept the idiosyncrasies of others. If you are patient with yourself, you will almost certainly be more tolerant toward your loved ones. If you have learned to forgive yourself, you're likely to find you can more easily forgive someone else. Self-respect increases as you stay committed to gaining a heart of wisdom. This attitude splashes onto your other relationships, and acceptance gradually becomes a way of life.

Father, let me see myself as You see me.
I'm covered with the righteousness of Christ.
I'm forgiven, free, and dearly loved. Help me
extend this mindset to those around me.

Object of Faith

"And as Moses lifted up the serpent in the wilderness, even so must the Son of Man be lifted up, that whoever believes in Him should not perish but have eternal life."

JOHN 3:14–15 NKJV

When Nicodemus inquires of Jesus how a man receives eternal life, Jesus recalls this Old Testament image. Knowing He would be lifted up on a cross, the Lord Jesus points Nicodemus and us to faith in Him alone. We must repent of our sin and believe in the Son of God who died on the cross. Sin and its consequences are around us like serpents, but into the midst of our fallen world God has sent Jesus to save us. He is the object of our faith. The crucified and resurrected Christ is the answer. He is the truth, the way, and the life.

Father, fix my gaze on Your Son lifted up for me.

Never Forgotten

The Lord will keep you from all harm—he will
watch over your life; the Lord will watch over your
coming and going both now and forevermore.
PSALM 121:7–8 NIV

Our lives are like an ancient city contained within walls. In an ancient city, the gatekeeper's job was to make decisions about what went in and out of the city. God is the gatekeeper of our lives. He is always watching, always guarding, and always vigilantly caring for us, even when we are least aware that He is doing so. Proverbs 2:8 (NKJV) says, "He guards the paths of justice, and preserves the way of His saints." By sending His Son to save us and His Spirit to dwell in us, He has assured us that we are never forgotten and never alone.

Forgive me, Father, for how often I forget
about You. Help me remember that You are
guarding and preserving me and that nothing
comes into my life without Your permission.

Closer. . .

*Thou hast also given me the shield of thy
salvation: and thy right hand hath holden me
up, and thy gentleness hath made me great.*
PSALM 18:35 KJV

A children's fable describes the sun and wind making a bet:
Who can get a man to take off his coat? The wind blows with
vengeance, using his strength to try and force the man's hand. The
sun simply shines, gently inviting the man to shed what he no
longer needs. God does the same with us. His gentleness warms
us toward love and faith. The closer we draw to God, the more
we'll treat others as He's treated us.

Father, fill me with Your love and gentleness.
Change my motives and actions to match the fruit
of Your Spirit. Draw me closer to Your heart.

Promises of God

*"For the LORD your God is living among you.
He is a mighty savior. He will take delight in you
with gladness. With his love, he will calm all your
fears. He will rejoice over you with joyful songs."*

ZEPHANIAH 3:17 NLT

Look at all the promises packed into this one verse of scripture! God is with you. He is your mighty Savior. He delights in you with gladness. He calms your fears with His love. He rejoices over you with joyful songs. Wow! What a bundle of hope is found here for the believer. Like a mother attuned to her newborn baby's cries, so is your heavenly Father's heart for you. He delights in being your Father. You are blessed to be a daughter of the King.

**Father, thank You for loving me the way
You do. You are all I need. Amen.**

Consistency

*I will behave myself wisely in a perfect way.
O when wilt thou come unto me? I will walk
within my house with a perfect heart.*
PSALM 101:2 KJV

Chameleons may be interesting to watch on the nature channel, but they're not something worth emulating in terms of character. Consistency in the way we live our lives—whether we're on the job, at home with family, or out on the town with friends—is a hallmark of integrity. If how we act is dependent on who we're with, we may be seeking the approval of others more than seeking God. In terms of integrity, whose approval are you seeking today?

Lord, help me to always be true to You and to myself. I want to look in the mirror each day knowing that I'm honoring You in all my words and deeds.

Into the Light

*Thou hast turned for me my mourning into
dancing: thou hast put off my sackcloth,
and girded me with gladness.*
PSALM 30:11 KJV

Some seasons of life pull you into the shadows. But God wants to help you make your way back into the light not because you shouldn't mourn, but because every season heralds a new beginning. There is joy ahead, even if you can't see it or feel it right now. Each day brings you closer to those first flutters of joy. Watch for them. Wait for them. Pray for them. Then celebrate their arrival with thanks and praise.

Father, I ask that You fill my heart and my home with joy! Let the season of joy return to my family. Thank You for pouring the fruits of Your Spirit into my heart.

Live, Love, Grow

When I said, My foot slippeth;
thy mercy, O LORD, held me up.
PSALM 94:18 KJV

There's safety in planting yourself in a recliner and interacting with the world via big-screen television. No real relationships to let you down or challenge you to grow up. Nothing to risk, so no chance to fail. But nowhere in scripture do we see inaction as God's plan for our lives. We're designed to live, love, and grow. Along the way, we'll also fall. It's part of being human. God's mercy gives us the courage to risk trying again.

Father, I'm a little scared to carry out Your plans for my life. Will You give me strength and courage to do Your will? I need You every moment.

Get Above It All

Set your minds on things above, not on earthly things.
COLOSSIANS 3:2 NIV

Sometimes the most difficult challenges you face play out in your head—where a struggle to control the outcome and work out the details of life can consume you. Once removed—far away from the details—you can see things from a higher perspective. Close your eyes and push out the thoughts that try to grab you and keep you tied to the things of the world. Reach out to God and let your spirit soar. Give your concerns to Him and let Him work out the details. Rest in Him and He'll carry you above it all, every step of the way.

God, You are far above any detail of life
that concerns me. Help me to trust You
today for answers to those things that
seem to bring me down. I purposefully set
my heart and mind on You today.

You're a Star!

*The ways of right-living people glow with light;
the longer they live, the brighter they shine.*
PROVERBS 4:18 MSG

Aging isn't for wimps! It's true. Whether you're twenty-five or seventy-five, there are probably things about getting older that you don't appreciate. Extra pounds. Hormone imbalances. Another gray hair. Yet, as a God-honoring woman, you probably have one thing that only grows more beautiful and amazing with age—a heart of wisdom. The longer you live and the more wisdom you accumulate, the brighter your influence. So congratulate yourself. You're not a wimp, you're a star.

Father, thank You for choosing me to be Your light
while I walk this earth. Let me radiate Your love
and goodness to others all the days of my life.

Glorious

The glory of the young is their strength;
the gray hair of experience is the splendor of the old.
PROVERBS 20:29 NLT

The expression "generation gap" became popular in the 1960s, although it probably existed in some uncoined sense throughout history. Young people don't get their grandparents, and the over-fifty crowd can't figure out their juniors. Some sense a standoff. But the truth is, there is beauty on both sides of the gap. Young people possess stamina and a lust for life, while those who've been around awhile are reservoirs of experience and wisdom. In God, we are glorious at any age.

Lord God, allow me to see the hearts of all people instead of our differences. Help me move boldly toward everyone You put on my path no matter their age or stage in life.

Use Your Gift

Each of you has been blessed with one of
God's many wonderful gifts to be used in the
service of others. So use your gift well.
1 PETER 4:10 CEV

God did not give you your talents for your own pleasure only.
These skills you have were meant to be offered to the world. He
wants to use them to build His kingdom here on earth. So pick up
your skill, whatever it is, and use it to bring grace to someone's life.

———————————

Lord, thank You for the blessing of Your
wonderful gifts. Help me to identify the gifts
You have given me, and help me to use them
well to bless others and honor You. Amen.

Cultivating Beauty

Humans are satisfied with whatever looks
good; GOD probes for what is good.
PROVERBS 16:2 MSG

Like many women, you probably enjoy looking nice when you go
out for a special occasion. You want a hairstyle that flatters your
face, clothes that fit well, and a little makeup to enhance your eyes
and cheeks. God likes it when you feel good about your appearance.
Still, He cares more about the inner you. He wants to cultivate
what's good about you socially, emotionally, mentally, and spiritually. Join with Him in cultivating the beauty that's inside you.

You created me in Your image, God,
and I'm so thankful! Let the glow on my face
and the twinkle in my eyes come from a heart
that knows Your love and faithfulness.

Today—and Tomorrow

*You are my strong shield, and I trust you
completely. You have helped me, and I will
celebrate and thank you in song.*

PSALM 28:7 CEV

God proves Himself to us over and over again. And yet over and over we doubt His power. We need to learn from experience. The God whose strength rescued us yesterday and the day before will certainly rescue us again today. As we celebrate the grace we received yesterday and the day before, we gain confidence and faith for today and tomorrow.

My Father, my strong shield, You have proven Yourself
to me repeatedly. Remind me of Your goodness.
I praise You and celebrate Your faithfulness. Amen.

God's Artwork

He telleth the number of the stars;
he calleth them all by their names.
PSALM 147:4 KJV

Like a child who carefully chooses the silver crayon to draw the dog with stars for eyes, God's artwork is an expression of who He is. It displays His creativity, attention to detail, love of diversity, meticulous organization, and even His sense of humor. Taking time to contemplate the beauty and complexity of nature can help paint a clearer picture for you of what God is like. He's an artist, as well as a Father, Savior, and friend.

I love looking at Your handiwork, Lord.
Your creativity shows how amazing and real You
are. Help me never take Your creation for granted.

Prayer Schedule

Seven times a day I praise you for your righteous laws.
PSALM 119:164 NIV

The Bible tells us to pray without ceasing. A fixed-hour prayer ritual is called "praying the hours" or the "daily office." Hearts and minds turn toward God at set times. We try to create a space in our busy lives to praise God and express our gratitude throughout the day.

We can create any kind of prayer schedule. Each stoplight we pass, the ring of the alarm on our watches, or a pause during television commercials can all serve as simple reminders to pray. We can be alert during the day for ways God protects and guides us.

Seven moments a day—to thank the Lord for all the moments of our lives.

Sometimes I forget to pray; busyness gets
in the way. But I can change that! I will set
aside specific times throughout my day to
pray and praise You, Lord. Amen.

The Lord Himself Goes Before You

"The LORD himself goes before you and will be with you; he will never leave you nor forsake you. Do not be afraid; do not be discouraged."

DEUTERONOMY 31:8 NIV

Joshua 1:9 tells us to "be strong and courageous. Do not be afraid; do not be discouraged, for the LORD your God will be with you wherever you go." Be encouraged! Even when it feels like it, you are truly never alone and never without access to God's power. If you've trusted Christ as your Savior, the Spirit of God Himself is alive and well and working inside you at all times. What an astounding miracle! The Creator of the universe dwells within you and is available to encourage you and help you make right choices on a moment-by-moment basis.

Thank You, Lord, for the incredible gift of Your presence in each and every situation I face. Allow me to remember this and to call upon Your name as I go about each day.

Pure Motives

We justify our actions by appearances;
God examines our motives.
PROVERBS 21:2 MSG

People—women and men—want to look good to others. Sometimes we do this by name-dropping, pretending we don't need help, or reciting our credentials and achievements. At other times we do it by being overly nice, overworking, and rarely saying no. Both approaches to trying to keep our appearances up can wear us out. Relief comes when you admit your need, allow God to purify your motives, and then just enjoy honoring Him as the person He created you to be.

God, I ask You to examine my heart. Show me anything that is hindering me from a more authentic relationship with You and those around me. I want to honor You!

On Truth's Side

We're rooting for the truth to win out in you.
We couldn't possibly do otherwise.
2 Corinthians 13:8 msg

As we look at the world around us, we can see that people often prefer falsehoods to truth. They choose to live in a world that soothes their anxiety rather than face life's reality. We cannot force people to acknowledge what they don't want to face, but we can do all we can to encourage them and build them up. We can cheer for the truth, trusting that God's grace is always on truth's side.

Father, author of truth, open my eyes to the truth of Your Word. Help me not to be swayed by falsehood but instead to cling to Your truth. Amen.

Be Anxious for Nothing

*Be anxious for nothing, but in everything by
prayer and supplication, with thanksgiving,
let your requests be made known to God.*
PHILIPPIANS 4:6 NKJV

"Be anxious for nothing" sounds like great advice, but at times most of us have the feeling that it only works for highly mature saints and is not practical for the average Christian.

Yet the key to making it work is found in the same verse: we can "be anxious for nothing" if we are continually taking those problems to God in prayer, thanking Him for solving past problems, and trusting Him to work the current situation out. Praying about things, of course, shouldn't keep us from doing what God inspires us to do to solve the problems. But we should trust and pray instead of fretting and worrying.

Father, anxiety makes me weary. Today I ask You to take all my problems and work them out for my good. Show me the way, Lord, and I will obey You. Amen.

More Than You Know

The LORD directs our steps, so why try to
understand everything along the way?
PROVERBS 20:24 NLT

Are you tired of trying so hard to make sure you do everything just right? Do you long to hear God whispering that He's with you and in control? Then you're like many other busy and over-worked women. God knows your desire to love others, serve, and make wise choices. He hears your genuine prayer for help and strength. And He's answering. So lean back and take a deep breath. You are loved more than you'll ever know.

Please increase my faith, Lord. I want to believe that
You are who You say You are! You are with me and
guiding me with each step. Help me trust You more.

Most Important

Tune your ears to the world of Wisdom;
set your heart on a life of Understanding.
PROVERBS 2:2 MSG

What do you listen to most? Do you hear the world's voice, telling you to buy, buy, buy; to dress and look a certain way; to focus on things that won't last? Or have you tuned your ears to hear the quiet voice of God's wisdom? You can tell the answer to that question by your response to yet another question: What is most important to you? Things? Or the intangible grace of true understanding?

Lord, You are wisdom. Tune my heart to Your wise voice. Make Your priorities my priorities, and fill my heart with Your wisdom and Your understanding. Amen.

Something from Nothing

By the word of the LORD were the heavens made;
and all the host of them by the breath of his mouth.
PSALM 33:6 KJV

Genesis tells us how God spoke nothing into something. But that "something" was not just anything. It was the divine artwork of creation. All of creation, from the tiniest microbe to the most expansive nebula, is wonderful in the fullest sense of the word. Take time to appreciate the wonder God has woven into the world. Take a walk in a park. Fill a vase with fresh flowers. Pet a puppy. Plant a petunia. Then, thank God.

Thank You for allowing us to spend time in Your wonderful creation, Lord God! I'm so amazed by You and Your divine artwork. Thank You, God!

Give Your Doubt Away

*The Lord will be your confidence and will
keep your foot from being caught.*
PROVERBS 3:26 NRSV

Life is risky. With these risks come adventure, fulfillment—and
uncertainty. Are you starting a career and overwhelmed with all
you must learn? Are you a new mother, wondering how you'll
raise this tiny person who awakens you in the night? Although
you enjoy your independence, do you wonder whether you'll ever
find a mate? Are you facing big decisions now that your husband
is gone? Whatever your challenge, give your doubt to God. He'll
never leave you. Never.

I lay my doubts at Your feet today, Lord. I want You
to be the Lord of my life. Not just my Savior but my
counselor, my ever-present friend, and my safe haven.

Be Authentic

*The LORD looks deep inside people and
searches through their thoughts.*
PROVERBS 20:27 NCV

If you're like most women who've participated in relationship sur-
veys, you want someone to hear your heart and not be frightened
off. Although you've been disappointed in relationships before,
you still desire to be loved for who you really are. Good news!
God is not surprised by what you feel, say, or think. He knows
you inside and out and loves you just the way you are. So drop
your guard and be authentic with Him. He isn't going anywhere.

I'm amazed that You see me, God! You are
at work in my heart and know me better
than I know myself. Continue to show me
who You are as I open my heart to You.

Thy Will Be Done

*He went away a second time and prayed,
"My Father, if it is not possible for this cup to be taken
away unless I drink it, may your will be done."*
MATTHEW 26:42 NIV

Jesus didn't just ask this just once—He made this request three times in Matthew 26. These red-letter prayers reveal the 100 percent human side of Jesus.

In one of His darkest hours, Jesus was overwhelmed with trouble and sorrow. He asked God for something that God would not provide. But Jesus, perfect and obedient, ended His prayers by saying, "*Your* will be done."

When we face our darkest hours, will we follow Jesus' example? Can we submit to God's perfect will, focusing on how much He loves us, even when His will doesn't match ours?

I wonder why You refuse when I ask for what I think is right. But Your knowledge is greater than my understanding. So, Thy will be done, God, Thy perfect will be done. Amen.

Never Bought

They trust in their riches and brag about all their
wealth. You cannot buy back your life or pay off God!
PSALM 49:6–7 CEV

We humans are easily confused about what real wealth is. We think that money can make us strong. We assume that physical possessions will enhance our importance and dignity in others' eyes. But life is not for sale, and grace can never be bought.

Heavenly Father, I am tempted to trust in worldly
riches, but I know they will never truly satisfy.
Help me to long for true wealth, which lies in
the promise of eternal life with You. Amen.

The Bigger Picture

"But you, be strong and do not lose courage,
for there is a reward for your work."
2 CHRONICLES 15:7 NASB

Why do you work? For a paycheck? For respect? For a sense of self-worth? All of those things are good reasons to work, but never forget that your work is part of a bigger picture. God wants to use your hands, intelligence, and efforts to build His kingdom, the place where grace dwells.

Father, help me to be strong, fill me with courage, and give me confidence in knowing that You will reward my work. I commit all I do to You. Amen.

Grounded in Love

"You'll be built solid, grounded in righteousness,
far from any trouble—nothing to fear!"
ISAIAH 54:14 MSG

Balance isn't something we can achieve in ourselves. Just when we think we have it all together, life tends to come crashing down around our ears. But even in the midst of life's most chaotic moments, God gives us grace; He keeps us balanced in His love. Like a building built to sway in an earthquake without falling down, we will stay standing if we remain grounded in His love.

———————————

Heavenly Father, keep me grounded in Your love. Provide for me a strong foundation to keep me stable through life's most chaotic moments. Thank You for Your steady hand. Amen.

Before Time

But I am like a green olive tree in the house of God:
I trust in the mercy of God for ever and ever.
PSALM 52:8 KJV

How do you love someone you can't see, hear, or touch? The same way you love an unborn child. You learn everything you can about what that child is like. You speak to it, even though it doesn't speak back. When you finally meet face-to-face, you find you're already in love. Yes, you can love someone you cannot yet see. As for God, His love for you transcends eternity. You're the child He's loved since before there was time.

Lord, prepare my heart to live in relationship
with You all the days of my life. I love You,
and I want to learn how to show my love for You.

Conversation of Prayer

But I have trusted in thy mercy; my heart shall rejoice in thy salvation. I will sing unto the LORD, because he hath dealt bountifully with me.
PSALM 13:5–6 KJV

When we pray, we expect things to happen—and they do. Inviting the Creator of the universe to be intimately involved in the details of our day is a mysterious and miraculous undertaking. But prayer isn't a tool. It's a conversation. God is not our almighty personal planner, helping us manage our lives more efficiently. He's someone who loves us. When you pray, remember you're speaking to someone who enjoys you as well as takes care of you.

———————————

Lord, please forgive me for treating You like a personal assistant instead of the Creator of all and the lover of my soul. I want to show my love for You.

Ask Him

People's thoughts can be like a deep well, but someone with understanding can find the wisdom there.
PROVERBS 20:5 NCV

People have their own answers—or can at least find them. This is a basic tenet of the highly successful industry of life coaching. Life coaches ask powerful questions that help their clients discover those hidden answers, move past their status quo, and grow. You have your own answers too. They may be lodged deep within you, but with some authentic sharing and a wise companion's thoughtful probing, you can find the wisdom. Ask God to direct you to this kind of authenticity.

You are my counselor and my source of wisdom, Lord. Reveal the thoughts and attitudes of my heart so that I can grow in truth and freedom.

Discover Balance

*Do you like honey? Don't eat too
much, or it will make you sick!*
PROVERBS 25:16 NLT

"All work and no play makes Jack a dull boy." (By the way, all work
and no play can make Jill a dull girl as well!) You've probably
heard this age-old axiom countless times. Yet the opposite is
also true. All play and no work makes Jack and Jill uninteresting,
not to mention unproductive. Focusing on one area of life to
the detriment of its counterpoint is not wise. You can discover
balance and thrive.

Lord, align my heart with Your will for my life.
Help me to find the balance I need to live a
meaningful and productive life as I follow You.

A Special Kind of Grace

*Oh, how blessed are you parents, with your quivers
full of children! Your enemies don't stand a chance
against you; you'll sweep them right off your doorstep.*
PSALM 127:4–5 MSG

What are your worst enemies? Despair? Self-doubt? Selfishness?
We all face enemies like these. But God's grace comes to us in
a special way through children. As we love them, we find hope;
we focus outward and forget about ourselves. And somehow
those funny little people manage to sweep our enemies right
off the doorsteps of our hearts!

Heavenly Father, thank You for the blessing of
little children. Thank You for the way they bring
hope and simplicity to my life, putting even my
darkest circumstances in perspective. Amen.

His Time, His Way

*Rest in the LORD, and wait patiently for
him: fret not thyself because of him who
prospereth in his way, because of the man
who bringeth wicked devices to pass.*

PSALM 37:7 KJV

When we encounter conflict or injustice, we want resolution.
We want relationships to be mended and wrongs to be made
right. We want villains to pay and victims to heal. Now. Wanting
this life to resemble heaven is a God-given desire. But the fact
is, we're not home yet. If you're impatient for a situation to
change, pray for perspective, do what you can, then trust God
for resolution in His time and in His way.

Lord, please give me Your perspective while I'm here
on earth. Some situations and conflicts simply baffle
me. I lift my cares into Your loving, capable hands.

Safe in Christ

*This is what God commands: that we believe
in his Son, Jesus Christ, and that we love
each other, just as he commanded.*
1 JOHN 3:23 NCV

Again and again, the Bible links faith and love. Our human tendency is to put up walls of selfishness around ourselves, to protect ourselves at all costs. God asks us instead to believe daily that we are safe in Christ and to allow ourselves to be vulnerable as we reach out in love to those around us.

Father God, Your commands are not
burdensome. You ask me to believe in Your
Son and to love others. Give me the grace
to obey You with all my heart. Amen.

Choose Grace

*And a servant of the Lord must not quarrel but must
be kind to everyone, a good teacher, and patient.*
2 TIMOTHY 2:24 NCV

Some days we can't help but feel irritated and out of sorts. But
no matter how we feel on the inside, we can choose our outward
behavior. We can make the decision to let disagreements go, to
refuse to argue, to act in kindness, to show patience and a willingness to listen (even when we feel impatient). We can choose
to walk in grace.

Lord, help me to be kind to everyone, to be a good
teacher, and to be patient with others. Thank You for
Your grace that allows me to be Your servant. Amen.

Capable Woman

She gets up before dawn to prepare breakfast for her household and plan the day's work for her servant girls.
PROVERBS 31:15 NLT

You've got a lot to do. Each of your roles shouts for attention. How can you do it all? You can't. You're only one woman, although a caring, capable one. As a new employee, first-time mother, or start-up business owner, you encounter huge learning curves. You'll need to adjust. You may need to wake up early or ask for specialized help. This phase won't last forever. Give yourself a break. Do what you need to do to maintain balance.

Your Word tells me that You've given me everything I need for life and godliness. It's through Your power alone that I can accomplish what You've set before me.

Lovely Wisdom

*"She'll garland your life with grace,
she'll festoon your days with beauty."*
PROVERBS 4:9 MSG

You are a beautiful creation of God. As a woman with a heart for God, you seek wisdom and understanding, and it shows. Grace reflects in your eyes as you speak with kindness and encouragement. Magazine advertisements and Hollywood may tell you that to be one of the "beautiful people" you must maintain an ideal weight, banish wrinkles, schedule regular pedicures, highlight your hair—and more. While all these regimens are fine, wisdom's loveliness in you far exceeds them all.

Fill my heart with radiance that comes from
Your love, Lord God. I ask for wisdom and grace
to be the beauty that others see in me.

Praiseworthy Woman

Charm is deceitful and beauty is passing, but a
woman who fears the Lord, she shall be praised.
PROVERBS 31:30 NKJV

Do you ever feel society's pressure to look younger than your years? Dress in the season's latest fashions? Be your neighborhood's most charming hostess? Perhaps you sense this pressure and so you keep trying. Or maybe you've given up. Surely you've noticed that birthdays are inevitable, outer beauty can fade, and charm can fool. But be encouraged today. As you continue to honor, respect, and love God, you become a praiseworthy woman. Are you smiling yet?

Lord, make me truly thankful for the woman
that You created me to be. Let me live to praise
You, heavenly Father. I delight myself in You.

Life's Circumstances

*My child, do not reject the LORD's discipline, and don't
get angry when he corrects you. The LORD corrects those
he loves, just as parents correct the child they delight in.*
PROVERBS 3:11–12 NCV

God doesn't send us to time-out, and He certainly doesn't take
us over His knee and spank us. Instead, His discipline comes to
us through the circumstances of life. By saying yes to whatever
we face, no matter how difficult and frustrating it may be, we
allow God's grace to infuse each moment of our day. We may be
surprised to find that even in life's most discouraging moments,
God's love was waiting all along.

Father, it can be difficult to accept Your
discipline. Help me to recognize when You are
correcting me and to see it as an outpouring
of Your love and Your delight. Amen.

No Division

In Christ's family there can be no division
into Jew and non-Jew, slave and free,
male and female. Among us you are all equal.
GALATIANS 3:28 MSG

Grace is a gift that none of us deserves, and by grace Jesus has removed all barriers between God and ourselves. God asks that as members of His family we also knock down all the walls we've built between ourselves and others. Not just the obvious ones, but also the ones that may hide in our blind spots. In Christ, there is no liberal or conservative, no educated or uneducated, no division whatsoever.

God, Your Son broke down all the walls.
I am so grateful that there is no longer any
division among Your children. Thank You for
making us all equal in Your sight. Amen.

Hungry

You serve me a six-course dinner right in
front of my enemies. You revive my drooping
head; my cup brims with blessing.
PSALM 23:5 MSG

At the end of a long day, do you ever feel weak and ravenous with hunger? You've gone too long without eating, and now your body demands food! We often do the same thing to our spirits, depriving them of the spiritual nourishment they need—and then we wonder why life seems so overwhelming and bleak. But dinner is on the table, and God is waiting to revive us with platefuls of grace and cups brimming with blessings.

Father, I am so grateful that You know all of my needs before I even ask. Thank You for reviving me and for filling my cup with overflowing blessings. Amen.

Everyone

If your enemy is hungry, feed him.
If he is thirsty, give him a drink.
PROVERBS 25:21 NCV

It's easy to have our friends over for dinner. Offering our hospitality to the people who give us pleasure is not much of a hardship. But hospitality gets harder when we offer it to the people who hurt our feelings, the people we really don't like very much. But God calls us to reach out in practical, tangible ways to everyone. Seek His grace to do this in some way every day.

Father, give me grace to love my enemies.
Empower me to offer them the nourishment of
Your love and the comfort of Your forgiveness,
knowing that it leads me closer to You. Amen.

Part of God's Plan

Mine eyes fail for thy salvation,
and for the word of thy righteousness.
PSALM 119:123 KJV

In an age of microwave meals, instant access, and ATMs, patience is fast becoming a lost virtue. Heaven forbid we're forced to wait in a drive-thru instead of ordering in the app and picking up right away! But waiting is part of God's plan. It takes time for babies to mature, for seasons to change, for fruit to ripen, and sometimes for prayers to be answered. Having to wait on God's timing reminds us that God is not our genie in a bottle. He's our sovereign Lord.

Help me wait on Your plans and Your timing,
Lord. I often trudge ahead on my own, and
that's when I fail the most. I need You, Jesus.

Perfect Blessing

The blessing of the LORD makes one rich.
PROVERBS 10:22 NKJV

God blesses His children. No doubt about it. Just look around you. Your life is richer because of His protection, provision, presence, grace, and love. How can you respond to God's blessing? Gratefully accept Him and all that He gives you. And then bless Him back. Perhaps that seems like the ultimate audacity. The perfect blesser receiving blessings from His own creation? Yet out of your rich inner resources of blessing, you can honor, revere, and bless the giver.

I bless Your name, heavenly Father! I praise and honor You for who You are and what You've done. I praise You for all the ways You've protected and led me. Thank You!

Build Up

By the blessing of the upright a city is exalted.
PROVERBS 11:11 NRSV

You may not know it, but you have the power to make a significant difference in your neighborhood, city, state, and—consequently—the world. What you believe about life; how you express those beliefs; how you treat your neighbors, acquaintances, government leaders, and coworkers reaches further than you may realize. When you bless those around you with your God-given wisdom, you are building up yourself, those around you, and gradually the world you live in.

Father, show me what it means to bring Your kingdom to others right here and now on this earth. You've given me much to do. Shine Your life and love through me.

Boundaries

"I, Wisdom, live together with good judgment. . . .
I was there when he set the limits of the seas,
so they would not spread beyond their boundaries."
PROVERBS 8:12, 29 NLT

Wisdom originates with God. When God designed the world, wisdom watched with joy as He drew distinct boundaries around the oceans and seas to protect His other creations from drowning. It's a picture of the boundaries He designed for you. You are not your mother. You are not your friend. You are not your spouse. No one has a right to step over your boundary line and take advantage of you. You are distinct. God made you that way.

Thank You for creating me so wonderfully
with distinct boundaries and purpose. My life
is Yours, Lord. Give me wisdom to interact
with others the way You designed me to.

Respond Wisely

*When you find a friend, don't outwear your welcome;
show up at all hours and he'll soon get fed up.*
PROVERBS 25:17 MSG

We all want to be loved and accepted. Yet some of us try too hard to make and keep friends. We may work harder than necessary to hold on to a boyfriend. We disregard boundaries, becoming overly enmeshed in another's life to the detriment of our own development. But there's good news. By placing your dependence on God first, you can change. Although transformation won't happen overnight, God will help you respond wisely to the people in your life. Just ask Him.

Jesus, help me take my cues from You in
relationships. Please help me to be wise
as I make and keep friendships. Infuse my
relationships with freedom, grace, and truth.

Reasonable?

"If you see your friend going wrong, correct him.
If he responds, forgive him. Even if it's personal against
you and repeated seven times through the day, and seven
times he says, 'I'm sorry, I won't do it again,' forgive him."
LUKE 17:3–4 MSG

As humans, we tend to feel that forgiveness has reasonable limits.
A person who repeats the same offense over and over can't be very
serious when he or she asks for forgiveness! It makes sense from
a human perspective. But fortunately for us, God isn't reasonable.
He forgives our sins no matter how many times we repeat them.
And He asks us to do the same for others.

Lord, I desperately need Your grace. Thank You for
offering me the gift of forgiveness over and over.
Help me to offer Your grace freely to others. Amen.

Peace of Heart

*Let them shout for joy, and be glad, that
favour my righteous cause: yea, let them say
continually, Let the Lord be magnified, which
hath pleasure in the prosperity of his servant.*

PSALM 35:27 KJV

The peace God pours out on those who follow Him runs deeper than peace of mind. It overflows into peace of heart. As you trust God a little more each day, placing the things you cherish most in His loving hands, you will release a need to control, a tendency toward worry, and a fear for the future. In their place, you will discover the comfort of being cared for like a child being held in a parent's nurturing embrace.

Forgive me for my control issues, Lord.
Help me trust You with each issue in my life,
knowing You are the source of all wisdom.

Rescued!

The LORD wants to show his mercy to you. He wants to rise and comfort you. The LORD is a fair God, and everyone who waits for his help will be happy.
ISAIAH 30:18 NCV

God doesn't want you to feel lonely and unhappy. He waits to bring you close to Him, to comfort you, to forgive you. Wait for Him to rescue you from life's unhappiness. His grace will never let you down. Keep your eyes fixed on Him, and you will find happiness again.

Lord, how I long to receive Your mercy. Draw near to me, rise up and comfort me, and give me happiness in knowing Your help will rescue me. Amen.

Choosing Cheerful

A cheerful disposition is good for your health;
gloom and doom leave you bone-tired.
Proverbs 17:22 MSG

Have you ever heard the saying "You may not be able to keep birds from perching on your head, but you can keep them from building nests in your hair"? It means we can't always control our emotions, but we can choose which ones we want to hold on to and dwell on. Choosing to be cheerful instead of gloomy is far healthier for our minds, bodies, and spirits. Being depressed is exhausting!

Father, when I am tempted to be gloomy and focus on negative thoughts, turn my heart around. Help me to focus on You, and fill my heart with cheer. Amen.

Scripture Index

OLD TESTAMENT

NEW TESTAMENT

Bible Permissions

Daily Inspiration for a Woman's Spirit!

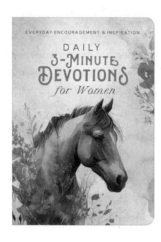

Daily 3-Minute Devotions for Women

This delightful daily devotional packs a powerful dose of comfort, encouragement, and inspiration into just-right-sized readings that will easily fit into your busy day. Each biblically faithful reading will speak to your heart and comfort your soul.

Flexible Casebound / 979-8-89151-022-7